PENGUIN BOOKS

500

MAJOR BARBARA

1905

SCREEN VERSION

1944

BY BERNARD SHAW

MAJOR BARBARA

A SCREEN VERSION

BY

BERNARD SHAW

PENGUIN BOOKS

HARMONDSWORTH · MIDDLESEX

First produced 1905 at the Court Theatre, London
First published in its original form as a stage play in 1907
Screened by Gabriel Pascal in 1940 and first shown in 1941
The screen version first published in Penguin Books in 1945
Reprinted 1949

MADE AND PRINTED IN GREAT BRITAIN
FOR PENGUIN BOOKS LTD
BY R. & R. CLARK, LTD, EDINBURGH

N.B.

This screen version of Major Barbara is not practicable for stage performance. The greater resources of the film, both financial and artistic, make it possible to take the spectators through the great Undershaft factory and industrial colony instead of putting them off with a spoken description ; and the same is true of half a dozen other scenes for which there is neither time nor money in theatres as distinct from cinemas.

The verses written to fit Rossini's once famous quartet from his *Moses in Egypt* were reset by Mr William Walton for Mr Pascal's film ; but I retain my first suggestion partly to explain the constrained versification imposed by Rossini's music ; partly because I must not infringe Mr Walton's copyright (Rossini's is extinct) ; and perhaps mainly because I feel sure that Undershaft was as old-fashioned in his musical taste as he was ultra-modern in his industrial management.

The passages quoted from Euripides are translated not by me, but by GILBERT MURRAY, whose English versions of the ancient Greek dramas had just come into our lives with all the impulsive power of original work shortly before Major Barbara was written. They tower above the best we were able to produce for ourselves in that period. My play stands indebted to Gilbert Murray in more ways than the way from Athens.

G. B. S.

a screen version of *Manon Lescaut* [illegible] not present in the performance. The greater resources of the film, both [illegible] and artistic, make it possible to take the spectators [illegible] the great [illegible] [illegible] and [illegible] instead of putting them off with a spoken description, and the same [illegible] of [illegible] other scenes [illegible] which [illegible] [illegible] more [illegible] distinct from cinema.

The [illegible] to a Russian [illegible] [illegible] [illegible] by Mr. [illegible] [illegible] partly to explain [illegible] [illegible] [illegible] by [illegible] music; partly [illegible] not [illegible] Mr. Walton [illegible] and partly because I feel sure that [illegible] [illegible] [illegible] as he was [illegible] [illegible] [illegible].

The [illegible] from [illegible] [illegible] [illegible] [illegible] [illegible] [illegible] [illegible] into our lives [illegible] [illegible] [illegible] [illegible] [illegible] [illegible] the [illegible] [illegible] [illegible] [illegible] [illegible] [illegible] [illegible] [illegible] that they are not [illegible].

C. [illegible]

PREFACE TO MAJOR BARBARA

The Gospel of St Andrew Undershaft

In the millionaire Undershaft I have represented a man who has become intellectually and spiritually as well as practically conscious of the irresistible natural truth which we all abhor and repudiate: to wit, that the greatest of our evils, and the worst of our crimes is poverty, and that our first duty, to which every other consideration should be sacrificed, is not to be poor. "Holy poverty," "poor but honest," "the respectable poor," and such phrases are as intolerable and as immoral as "drunken but amiable," "fraudulent but a good after-dinner speaker," "splendidly criminal," or the like. Security, the chief pretence of civilization, cannot exist where the worst of dangers, the danger of poverty, hangs over everyone's head, and where the alleged protection of our persons from violence is only an accidental result of the existence of a police force whose real business is to force the poor man to see his children starve whilst the money that might feed and clothe them goes to overfeed pet dogs.

It is difficult to make people realize that an evil is an evil. For instance, we seize a man and deliberately do him a malicious injury: say, imprison him for years. One would not suppose that it needed any exceptional clearness of wit to recognize in this an act of diabolical cruelty. But in England such a recognition provokes a stare of surprise, followed by an explanation that the outrage is punishment or justice or something else that is all right, or perhaps by a heated attempt to argue that we should all be robbed and murdered in our beds if such stupid villainies as sentences of imprisonment were not committed daily. It is useless to argue that even if this were true, which it is not, the alternative to adding crimes of our own to the crimes from which we suffer is not helpless submission. Chicken-pox is an evil; but if I were to declare that we must either submit to it or else repress it sternly by seizing everyone who suffers from it and punishing them by inoculation with smallpox, I should be laughed at ; for though nobody could deny that the result would be to prevent chickenpox to some extent by making people avoid it much more carefully, and to effect a further apparent prevention by making them conceal it very anxiously, yet people would have sense enough to see that the deliberate propagation of smallpox was a creation of evil, and must therefore be ruled out in favor of purely humane and hygienic measures. Yet in the precisely parallel case of a man breaking into my house and stealing my wife's diamonds I am expected as a matter of course to steal ten years of his life, torturing him all the time. If he tries to defeat that monstrous retaliation by shooting me, my survivors hang him. The net result suggested by the police statistics is that we inflict atrocious injuries on the burglars we catch in order to make the rest take effectual precautions against detection ; so that instead of saving our wives' diamonds from burglary we only greatly decrease our chances of ever getting them back, and increase our chances of being shot by the robber if we are unlucky enough to disturb him at his work.

But the thoughtless wickedness with which we scatter sentences of imprisonment, torture in the solitary cell and on the plank bed, privation of human intercourse and daily news, and flogging, on moral invalids and energetic rebels, is as nothing compared to the silly levity with which we tolerate poverty as if it were either a wholesome tonic for lazy people or else a virtue to be embraced as St Francis embraced it. If a man is indolent, let him be poor. If he is drunken, let him be poor. If he is not a gentleman, let him be poor. If he is addicted to the fine arts or to pure science instead of to trade and finance, let him be poor. If he chooses to spend his wages on his beer and his family instead of saving it up for his old age, let him be poor. Let nothing be done for " the undeserving " : let him be poor. Serve him right ! Also—somewhat inconsistently—blessed are the poor !

Now what does this Let Him Be Poor mean ? It means let him be weak. Let him be ignorant. Let him become a nucleus of disease. Let him be a standing exhibition and example of ugliness and dirt. Let him have rickety children. Let him be cheap, and drag his fellows down to his own price by selling himself to do their work. Let his habitations turn our cities into poisonous congeries of slums. Let his daughters infect our young men with the diseases of the streets, and his sons revenge him by turning the nation's manhood into scrofula, cowardice, cruelty, hypocrisy, political imbecility, and all the other fruits of oppression and malnutrition. Let the undeserving become still less deserving; and let the deserving lay up for himself, not treasures in heaven, but horrors in hell upon earth. This being so, is it really wise to let him be poor? Would he not do ten times less harm as a prosperous burglar, incendiary, ravisher or murderer, to the utmost limits of humanity's comparatively negligible impulses in these directions? Suppose we were to abolish all penalties for such activities, and decide that poverty is the one thing we will not tolerate—that every adult with less than a thousand a year shall be painlessly but inexorably killed, and every hungry half naked child forcibly fattened and clothed, would not that be an enormous improvement on our existing system, which has already destroyed so many civilizations, and is visibly destroying ours? Surely the sensible course would be to give every man enough to live well on, so as to guarantee the community against the possibility of a case of the malignant disease of poverty, and then (necessarily) to see that he earned it.

Undershaft, the hero of Major Barbara, is a man who, having grasped the fact that poverty is a crime, knows that when society offered him the alternative of poverty or a lucrative trade in death and destruction, it offered him, not a choice between opulent villainy and humble virtue, but between energetic enterprise and cowardly infamy. His conduct stands the Kantian test, which Peter Shirley's does not. Peter Shirley is what we call the honest poor man. Undershaft is what we call the wicked rich one: Shirley is Lazarus, Undershaft Dives. Well, the misery of the world is due to the fact that the great mass of men act and believe as Peter Shirley acts and believes.

If they acted and believed as Undershaft acts and believes, the immediate result would be a revolution of incalculable beneficence. To have money, says Undershaft, is with me a point of honor for which I am prepared to kill to make my own life worth living. This preparedness is, as he says, the final test of sincerity. Like Froissart's medieval hero, who saw that "to rob and pill was a good life" he is not the dupe of that public sentiment against killing which is propagated and endowed by people who but for it would be killed themselves, or of the mouth-honor paid to poverty and obedience by rich and insubordinate parasites who want to rob the poor without courage and command them without superiority. Froissart's knight, in placing the achievement of a good life before all the other duties—which indeed are not duties at all when they conflict with it, but plain wickednesses—behaved bravely, admirably, and, in the final analysis, public-spiritedly. Medieval society, on the other hand, behaved very badly indeed in organizing itself so stupidly that a good life could be achieved by robbing and pilling. If the knight's contemporaries had been all as resolute as he, robbing and pilling would have been the shortest way to the gallows, just as, if we were all as resolute and clearsighted as Undershaft, an attempt to live by means of what is called "an independent income" would be the shortest way to the lethal chamber. But as, thanks to our political ignorance and personal cowardice (fruits of poverty, both), the best imitation of a good life now procurable is life on an independent income, all sensible people aim at securing such an income, and are, of course, careful to legalize and moralize both it and all the actions and sentiments which lead to it and support it as an institution. What else can they do? They know, of course, that they are rich because others are poor. But they cannot help that: it is for the poor to repudiate poverty when they have had enough of it. The thing can be done easily enough: the demonstrations to the contrary made by the economists, jurists, moralists and sentimentalists hired by the rich to defend them, or even doing the work gratuitously out of sheer folly and abjectness, impose only on those who have leisure to read, and want to be imposed on.

The reason why the independent income-tax payers are not solid in defence of their position is that the poverty of those we rob prevents our having the good life for which we sacrifice them. Rich men or aristocrats with a developed sense of life—men like Ruskin and William Morris and Kropotkin—have enormous social appetites and very fastidious personal ones. They are not content with handsome houses: they want handsome cities. They are not content with bediamonded wives and blooming daughters: they complain because the charwoman is badly dressed, because the laundress smells of gin, because the sempstress is anemic, because every man they meet is not a friend and every woman not a romance. They turn up their noses at their neighbor's drains, and are made ill by the architecture of their neighbor's house. Trade patterns made to suit vulgar people do not please them; and they can get nothing else. The very air is not good enough for them: there is too much factory smoke in it. They even demand abstract conditions: justice, honor, a healthy moral atmosphere, an honest nexus to replace the cash nexus. Finally they declare that though to rob and pill with your own hand on horseback and in steel coat may have been a good life, to rob and pill by the hands of the policeman, the bailiff, and the soldier, and to underpay them meanly for doing it, is not a good life, but rather fatal to all possibility of even a tolerable one. They call on the poor to revolt, and, finding the poor shocked at their ungentlemanliness, despairingly revile them for their "damned wantlessness" (*verdammte Bedürfnislosigkeit*).

So far, however, their attack on society has lacked simplicity. The poor do not share their tastes, nor understand their art-criticisms, nor want the simple life, the aesthetic life, the literate life: on the contrary, they want very much to wallow in all the costly vulgarities from which the elect souls among the rich turn away with loathing. It is by surfeit and not by abstinence that they will be cured of their hankering after unwholesome sweets. What they do dislike and are ashamed of is their poverty. To ask them to fight for the difference between the Picture Post and the Kelmscott Chaucer is silly: they prefer the Post. "Cease to be slaves, in order that you may become cranks" is not a very inspiring call to arms; nor is it really improved by substituting saints for cranks. Both terms denote men of genius; and the common man does not want to live the life of a saint or a man of genius. But he does want more money. Whatever else he may be vague about, he is clear about that. He may or may not prefer Major Barbara to the Drury Lane pantomime; but he always prefers a pound to five shillings.

Now to deplore this preference as sordid, and teach children that it is sinful to desire money, is to strain towards the extreme limit of impudence in lying and corruption in hypocrisy. The universal regard for money is the one hopeful fact in our civilization, the one sound spot in our social conscience. Money is the most important thing in the world. It represents health, strength, honor, generosity and beauty as conspicuously and undeniably as the want of it represents illness, weakness, disgrace, meanness and ugliness. Not the least of its virtues is that it destroys base people as certainly as it fortifies and dignifies noble people. It is only when it is cheapened to worthlessness for some and made impossibly dear to others, that it becomes a curse. In short, it is a curse only in such foolish social conditions that life itself is a curse. For the two things are inseparable: money is the counter that enables life to be distributed socially: it *is* life as truly as gold coins and bank notes are money. The first duty of every citizen is to insist on having money on reasonable terms; and this demand is not complied with by giving four men a few shillings each for ten or twelve hours' drudgery and one man a thousand pounds for nothing. The crying need of the nation is not for better morals, cheaper bread, temperance, liberty, culture, redemption of fallen sisters and erring brothers, nor the grace, love and fellowship of the Trinity, but simply for enough money. And the evil to be attacked is not sin, suffering, greed, priestcraft, kingcraft, demagogy, monopoly, ignorance, drink, war, pestilence, nor any of the other consequences of poverty, but just poverty itself.

Once take your eyes from the ends of the earth and fix them on this truth just under your nose; and Andrew Undershaft's views will not perplex you in the least. Unless indeed his constant sense that he is only the instrument of a Will or Life Force which uses him for purposes wider than his own, may puzzle you. If so, that is because you are walking either in artificial Darwinian darkness, or in mere stupidity. All genuinely religious people have that consciousness. To them Undershaft the Mystic will be quite intelligible, and his perfect comprehension of his daughter the Salvationist and her lover the Euripidean Republican natural and inevitable. This, however, is not new, even on the stage. What is new, as far as I know, is that article in Undershaft's religion which recognizes in Money the first need, and in poverty the vilest sin of man and society.

This dramatic conception has not, of course, been reached in one step. Nor has it been borrowed from Nietzsche nor from any man born beyond the Channel. The late Samuel Butler, in his own department the greatest English writer of the latter half of the XIX century, steadily inculcated the necessity and morality of a conscientious Laodiceanism in religion and of an earnest and constant sense of the importance of money. It drives one almost to despair of English literature that when I produced plays in which Butler's extraordinarily fresh, free and future-piercing suggestions had an obvious share, I was reproached for echoing Schopenhauer, Ibsen, and Nietzsche. Really, the English do not deserve to have great men. They allowed Butler to die practically unknown whilst in Sicily there was already a Via Samuele Butler. When English tourists came upon it they asked either "Who the devil was Samuele Butler?" or wondered why the Sicilians should perpetuate the memory of the author of Hudibras.

MAJOR BARBARA

The Salvation Army

When Major Barbara was produced in London, the second act was reported in an important northern newspaper as a withering attack on the Salvation Army, and the despairing ejaculation of Barbara deplored by a London daily as a tasteless blasphemy. And they were set right, not by the professed critics of the theatre, but by religious and philosophical publicists who not only understood the act as well as the Salvationists themselves, but also saw it in its relation to the religious life of the nation : a life which then lay not only outside the sympathy of many theatre critics, but outside their knowledge of society. Indeed nothing could be more ironically curious than the confrontation Major Barbara effected of the theatre enthusiasts with the religious enthusiasts. On the one hand was the playgoer, always seeking pleasure, paying exorbitantly for it, suffering unbearable discomforts for it, and not always getting it. On the other hand was the Salvationist, repudiating gaiety, courting effort and sacrifice, yet always in the wildest spirits, laughing, joking, singing, rejoicing, drumming, and tambourining : his life flying by in a flash of excitement, and his death arriving as a climax of triumph. And, if you please, the playgoer despising the Salvationist as a joyless person, shut out from the heaven of the theatre, self-condemned to a life of hideous gloom ; and the Salvationist mourning over the playgoer as over a prodigal with vine leaves in his hair, careering outrageously to hell amid the popping of champagne corks and the ribald laughter of sirens ! Could misunderstanding be more complete, or sympathy worse misplaced ?

Fortunately, the Salvationists are more accessible to the religious character of the drama than the playgoers to the gay energy and artistic fertility of religion. They can see, when it is pointed out to them, that a theatre, as a place where two or three are gathered togther, takes from that divine presence an inalienable sanctity of which the grossest and profanest farce can no more deprive it than a hypocritical sermon by a snobbish bishop can desecrate Westminster Abbey. But in our professional playgoers this indispensable preliminary conception of sanctity seems wanting. They talk of actors as mimes and mummers, and I fear, think of playwrights as liars and pandars whose main business is the voluptuous soothing of the tired city speculator when what he calls the serious business of the day is over. Passion, the life of drama, means nothing to them but primitive sexual excitement: such phrases as "impassioned poetry" or "passionate love of truth" have fallen quite out of their vocabulary and been replaced by "passional crime" and the like. They assume, as far as I can gather, that people in whom passion has a larger scope are passionless and therefore uninteresting. Consequently they come to think of religious people either as figures of fun or as hypocrites, bores, and spoilsports. And so, when Barbara cracks Salvation Army jokes, and snatches a kiss from her lover across his drum, the devotees of the theatre think they ought to appear shocked, and conclude that the whole play is an elaborate mockery of the Army. And then either hypocritically rebuke me for mocking, or foolishly take part in the supposed mockery!

Even the handful of mentally competent critics got into difficulties over my demonstration of the economic deadlock in which the Salvation Army finds itself. Some of them thought that the Army would not have taken money from a distiller and a cannon founder: others thought it should not have taken it: all assumed more or less definitely that it reduced itself to absurdity or hypocrisy by taking it. On the first point the reply of the Army itself was prompt and conclusive. As one of its officers said, they would take money from the devil himself and be only too glad to get it out of his hands and into God's. They gratefully acknowledged that publicans not only give them money but allow them to collect it in the bar, sometimes even when there is a Salvation meeting outside preaching teetotalism. In fact, they questioned the verisimilitude of the play, not because Mrs Baines took the money, but because Barbara refused it.

On the point that the Army ought not to take such

money, its justification is obvious. It must take the money because it cannot exist without money, and there is no other money to be had. Practically all the spare money in the country consists of a mass of rent, interest, and profit, every penny of which is bound up with crime, drink, prostitution, disease, and all the evil fruits of poverty, as inextricably as with enterprise, wealth, commercial probity, and national prosperity. The notion that you can earmark certain coins as tainted is childish. None the less the fact that all our money is tainted gives a very severe shock to earnest young souls when some dramatic instance of the taint first makes them conscious of it. When an enthusiastic young clergyman of the Established Church first realizes that the Ecclesiastical Commissioners receive the rents of sporting public houses, brothels, and sweating dens ; or that the most generous contributor at his last charity sermon was an employer trading in female labor cheapened by prostitution ; or that the only patron who can afford to rebuild his church or his schools or give his boys' brigade a gymnasium or a library is the son-in-law of a Chicago meat King, that young clergyman has, like Barbara, a very bad quarter hour. But he cannot help himself by refusing to accept money from anybody except sweet old ladies with independent incomes and gentle and lovely ways of life. He has only to follow up the income of the sweet ladies to its industrial source, and there he will find Mrs Warren's profession and all the rest of it. His own stipend has the same root. He must either share the world's guilt or go to another planet. He must save the world's honor if he is to save his own. This is what all the Churches find just as the Salvation Army and Barbara find it in the play. Her discovery is that she is her father's accomplice ; that the Salvation Army is the accomplice of the distiller and the dynamite maker ; that they can no more escape one another than they can escape the air they breathe ; and that there is no salvation for them through personal righteousness, but only through the redemption of the whole nation from its vicious, lazy, competitive anarchy. Nevertheless we proceed without the least misgiving as to the elevation of our private characters, the purity of our private atmospheres, and our right to repudiate as foreign to ourselves the coarse depravity of the garret and the slum. Not that we mean any harm: we only desire to be, in our little private way, ladies and gentlemen. We do not understand Barbara's lesson because we have not, like her, learnt it by taking our part in the larger life of the nation.

Barbara's Return to the Colors

Barbara's return to the colors may yet provide a subject for the dramatic historian of the future. To go back to the Salvation Army with the knowledge that even the Salvationists themselves are not saved yet; that poverty is not blessed, but a most damnable sin; and that when General Booth chose Blood and Fire for the emblem of Salvation instead of the Cross, he was perhaps better inspired than he knew: such knowledge, for the daughter of Andrew Undershaft, will clearly lead to something hopefuller than distributing bread and treacle at the expense of Bodger.

It is a very significant thing, this instinctive choice of the military form of organization, this substitution of the drum for the organ, by the Salvation Army. Does it not suggest that the Salvationists divine that they must actually fight the devil instead of merely praying at him? At present, it is true, they have not quite ascertained his correct address. When they do, they may give a very rude shock to that sense of security which he has gained from his experience of the fact that hard words, even when uttered by eloquent essayists and lecturers, or carried unanimously at enthusiastic public meetings on the motion of eminent reformers, break no bones. It has been said that the French Revolution was the work of Voltaire, Rousseau and the Encyclopedists. It seems to me to have been the work of men who had observed that virtuous indignation, caustic criticism, conclusive argument, and instructive pamphleteering, even when done by the most earnest and witty literary geniuses, were as useless as praying, things going steadily from bad to worse whilst Rousseau's Social Contract and the pamphlets of Voltaire were at the height of their vogue. Eventually, as we know, perfectly respectable citizens and earnest philanthropists connived at the September massacres because hard experience had convinced them that if they contented themselves with appeals to humanity and patriotism, the aristocracy, though it would read their appeals with the greatest enjoyment and appreciation, flattering and admiring the writers, would none the less continue to conspire with foreign monarchists to undo the revolution and restore the old system with every circumstance of savage vengeance and ruthless repression of popular liberties.

The nineteenth century saw the same lesson repeated in England. It had its Utilitarians, its Christian Socialists, its Fabians (still extant): it had Bentham, Mill, Dickens, Ruskin, Carlyle, Butler, Henry George, and Morris. And the end of all their efforts is the Chicago described by Mr Upton Sinclair, and the London in which the people who pay to be amused by my dramatic representation of Peter Shirley turned out to starve at forty because there are younger slaves to be had for his wages, do not take, and have not the slightest intention of taking, any effective step to organize society in such a way as to make that everyday infamy impossible. I, who have preached and pamphleteered like any Encyclopedist, have to confess that my methods are no use, and would be no use if I were Voltaire, Rousseau, Shelley, Bentham, Marx, Mill, Dickens, Carlyle, Ruskin, Butler, and Morris all rolled into one, with Euripides, Erasmus, More, Montaigne, Molière, Beaumarchais, Swift, Goethe, Wagner, Ibsen, Tolstoy, Jesus and the prophets all thrown in (as indeed in some sort I actually am, standing as I do on all their shoulders). The problem being to make heroes out of cowards, we paper apostles and artist-magicians have succeeded only in giving cowards all the sensations of heroes whilst they tolerate every abomination, accept every plunder, and submit to every oppression. Christianity, in making a merit of such submission, has marked only that depth in the abyss at which the very sense of shame is lost. The Christian has been like Dickens' doctor in the debtor's prison, who tells the newcomer of its ineffable peace and security: no duns, no tyrannical collectors of rates and taxes, no importunate hopes nor exacting duties, nothing but the rest and safety of having no farther to fall.

Yet in the poorest corner of this soul-destroying Christendom vitality suddenly begins to germinate again. Joyousness, a sacred gift long dethroned by the hellish laughter of derision and obscenity, rises like a flood miraculously out of the fetid dust and mud of the slums; rousing marches and impetuous dithyrambs rise to the heavens from people among whom the depressing noise called "sacred music" is a standing joke; a flag with Blood and Fire on it is unfurled, not in murderous rancor, but because fire is beautiful and blood a vital and splendid red; Fear, which we flatter by calling Self, vanishes; and transfigured men and women carry their gospel through a transfigured world, calling their leader General, themselves captains and brigadiers, and their whole body an Army: praying, but praying only for refreshment, for strength to fight, and for needful MONEY (a notable sign, that); preaching, but not preaching submission; daring ill-usage and abuse, but not putting up with more of it than is inevitable; and practising what the world will let them practise, including soap and water, color and music. There is danger in such activity; and where there is danger there is hope. Our present security is nothing, and can be nothing, but evil made irresistible.

WEAKNESSES OF THE SALVATION ARMY

For the present, however, it is not my business to flatter the Salvation Army. Rather must I point out to it that it has almost as many weaknesses as the Church of England itself. It is building up a business organization which will compel it eventually to see that its original staffs of enthusiast-commanders shall be succeeded by a bureaucracy of men of business. That has always happened sooner or later to great orders founded by saints ; and the order founded by Saint William Booth will not escape the same danger. It is even more dependent than the Church on rich people who would cut off supplies at once if it began to preach a revolt against poverty which must also be a revolt against riches. It is hampered by a heavy contingent of pious elders who are not really Salvationists at all, but Evangelicals of the old school. It still " sticks to Moses," which is flat nonsense at this time of day if it means, as I am afraid it does, that the Book of Genesis contains a trustworthy scientific account of the origin of species, and that the god to whom Jephthah sacrificed his daughter is any less obviously a tribal idol than Dagon or Chemosh.

Further, there is still too much other-worldliness about the Army. Like Frederick's grenadier, the Salvationist wants to live for ever (the most monstrous way of crying for the moon) ; and though it is evident to anyone who has ever heard General Booth and his best officers that they would work as hard for human salvation as they do at present if they believed that death would be the end of them individually, they and their followers have a bad habit of talking as if the Salvationists were heroically enduring a very bad time on earth as an investment which will bring them in dividends later on in the form, not of a better life to come for the whole world, but of an eternity spent by themselves personally in a sort of bliss which would bore any active person to a second death. Surely the truth is that the Salvationists are unusually happy people. And is it not the very diagnostic of true salvation that it shall overcome the fear of death ? Now the man who has come to believe that there is no such thing as death, the change so called being merely the transition to an exquisitely happy and utterly careless life, has not overcome the fear of death at all : on the contrary, it has overcome him so completely that he refuses to die on any terms whatever. I do not call a Salvationist really saved until he is ready to lie down cheerfully on the scrap heap, having paid scot and lot and something over, and let his eternal life pass on to renew its youth in the battalions of the future.

Then there is the nasty lying habit called confession, which the Army encourages because it lends itself to dramatic oratory, with plenty of thrilling incident. For my part, when I hear a convert relating the violences and oaths and blasphemies he was guilty of before he was saved, making out that he was a very terrible fellow then and is the most contrite and chastened of Christians now, I believe him no more than I believe the millionaire who says he came up to London or Chicago as a boy with only three half-pence in his pocket. Salvationists have said to me that Barbara in my play would never have been taken in by so transparent a humbug as Snobby Price ; and certainly I do not think Snobby could have taken in any experienced Salvationist on a point on which the Salvationist did not wish to be taken in. But on the point of conversion all Salvationists wish to be taken in ; for the more obvious the sinner the more obvious the miracle of his conversion. When converted burglars and reclaimed drunkards are the attractions at an experience meeting, the burglars can hardly be too burglarious or the drunkards too drunken. As long as such attractions are relied on, you will have your Snobbies claiming to have beaten their mothers when they were as a matter of prosaic fact habitually beaten by them, and your Rummies of the tamest respectability pretending to a past of reckless and dazzling vice. Even when confessions are sincerely autobiographic we should beware of assuming that the impulse to make them was pious or that the interest of the hearers is wholesome. As well might we assume that the poor people who insist on shewing disgusting ulcers to district visitors are convinced hygienists, or that the curiosity which sometimes welcomes such exhibitions is a pleasant and creditable one. One is often tempted to suggest that those who pester our police superintendents with confessions of murder might very wisely be taken at their word and executed, except in the few cases in which a real murderer is seeking to be relieved of his guilt by confession and expiation. For though I am not, I hope, an unmerciful person, I do not think that the inexorability of the deed once done should be disguised by any ritual, whether in the confessional or on the scaffold.

And here my disagreement with the Salvation Army, and with all propagandists of the Cross (which I loathe as I loathe all gibbets) becomes deep indeed. Forgiveness, absolution, atonement, are figments: punishment is only a pretence of cancelling one crime by another; and we can no more have forgiveness without vindictiveness than a cure without a disease. We shall never get a high morality from people who conceive that their misdeeds are revocable and pardonable, nor in a society where absolution and expiation are officially provided for us all. The demand may be very real; but the supply is spurious.

Thus Bill Walker, in my play, having assaulted the Salvation Lass, presently finds himself overwhelmed with an intolerable conviction of sin under the skilled treatment of Barbara. Straightway he begins to try to unassault the lass and deruffianize his deed, first by getting punished for it in kind, and, when that relief is denied him, by fining himself a pound to compensate the girl. He is foiled both ways. He finds the Salvation Army as inexorable as the facts. It will not punish him: it will not take his money. It will not tolerate a redeemed ruffian: it leaves him no means of salvation except ceasing to be a ruffian. In doing this, the Salvation Army instinctively grasps the central truth of Christianity and discards its central superstition: that central truth being the vanity of revenge and punishment, and that central superstition the salvation of the world by the gibbet.

For, be it noted, Bill has assaulted an old and starving woman also; and for this worse offence he feels no remorse whatever, because she makes it clear that her malice is as great as his own. "Let her have the law of me, as she said she would," says Bill: "what I done to her is no more on what you might call my conscience than sticking a pig." This shews a perfectly natural and wholesome state of mind on his part. The old woman, like the law she threatens him with, is perfectly ready to play the game of retaliation with him: to rob him if he steals, to flog him if he strikes, to murder him if he kills. By example and precept the law and public opinion teach him to impose his will on others by anger, violence, and cruelty, and to wipe off the moral score by punishment. That is sound Crosstianity. But this Crosstianity has got entangled with something which Barbara calls Christianity, and which unexpectedly causes her to refuse to play the hangman's game of Satan casting out Satan. She refuses to prosecute a drunken ruffian; she converses on equal terms with a blackguard to whom no lady should be seen speaking in the public street: in short, she imitates Christ. Bill's conscience reacts to this just as naturally as it does to the old woman's threats. He is placed in a position of unbearable moral inferiority, and strives by every means in his power to escape from it, whilst he is still quite ready to meet the abuse of the old woman by attempting to smash a mug on her face. And that is the triumphant justification of Barbara's Christianity as against our system of judicial punishment and the vindictive villain-thrashings and "poetic justice" of the romantic stage.

For the credit of literature it must be pointed out that the situation is only partly novel. Victor Hugo long ago gave us the epic of the convict and the bishop's candlesticks, of the Crosstian policeman annihilated by his encounter with the Christian Valjean. But Bill Walker is not, like Valjean, romantically changed from a demon into an angel. There are millions of Bill Walkers in all classes of society today; and the point which I, as a professor of natural psychology, desire to demonstrate, is that Bill, without any change in his character or circumstances whatsoever, will react one way to one sort of treatment and another way to another.

In proof I might point to the sensational object lesson provided by our commercial millionaires today. They begin as brigands: merciless, unscrupulous, dealing out ruin and death and slavery to their competitors and employees, and facing desperately the worst that their competitors can do to them. The history of the English factories, the American Trusts, the exploitation of African gold, diamonds, ivory and rubber, outdoes in villainy the worst that has ever been imagined of the buccaneers of the Spanish Main. Captain Kidd would have marooned a modern Trust magnate for conduct unworthy of a gentleman of fortune. The law every day seizes on scoundrels who are not capitalists and punishes them with a cruelty worse than their own, with the result that they come out of the torture house more dangerous than they went in, and renew their evil doing (nobody will employ them at anything else) until they are again seized, again tormented, and again let loose, with the same result.

But the moneyed scoundrel is dealt with very differently, and very Christianly. He is not only forgiven : he is idolized, respected, made much of, all but worshipped. Society returns him good for evil in the most extravagant overmeasure. And with what result ? He begins to idolize himself, to respect himself, to live up to the treatment he receives. He preaches sermons ; he writes books of the most edifying advice to young men, actually persuading himself that he got on by taking his own advice ; he endows educational institutions ; he supports charities ; he dies finally in the odor of sanctity, leaving a will which is a monument of public spirit and bounty. And all this without any change in his character. The spots of the leopard and the stripes of the tiger are as brilliant as ever ; but the conduct of the world towards him has changed ; and his conduct has changed accordingly. You have only to reverse your attitude towards him, to lay hands on his property, revile him, torture him, and he will be a brigand again in a moment, as ready to crush you as you are to crush him, and quite as full of pretentious moral reasons for doing it.

In short, when Major Barbara says that there are no scoundrels, she is right : there are no absolute scoundrels, though there are intolerable people of whom I shall treat presently. Every reasonable man (and woman) is a potential scoundrel and a potential good citizen. Whatever his character, what he does, and what we think of what he does, depend mostly on how we treat him. The characteristics that ruin a citizen in one class make him eminent in another.

The characters that behave differently in different circumstances behave alike in similar circumstances. Take a common English character like that of Bill Walker. We meet Bill everywhere: on the judicial bench, on the episcopal bench, in the Privy Council, at the War Office and Admiralty, as well as in the Old Bailey dock or in the ranks of casual unskilled labor. And the morality of Bill's characteristics varies with these various circumstances. The faults of the burglar are the qualities of the financier: the manners and habits of a duke would cost a city clerk his situation. In short, though character is independent of circumstances, conduct is not; and our moral judgments of character are not: both are circumstantial. Take any condition of life in which the circumstances are for a mass of men practically alike: prison, the peerage, the army, the factory, the stables, the gipsy encampment or where you please! In spite of diversity of character and temperament, the conduct and morals of the individuals in each group are as predicable and as alike in the main as if they were a flock of sheep, morals being mostly only social habits and circumstantial necessities. Strong people know this and count upon it. In nothing have the master-minds of the world been distinguished from the ordinary suburban season-ticket holder more than in their straightforward perception of the fact that mankind in the lump is a single species, and not a menagerie of gentlemen and bounders, villains and heroes, cowards and daredevils, peers and peasants, shopkeepers and aristocrats, artisans and laborers, washerwomen and duchesses, in which all the grades of income and caste represent distinct animals who must not be introduced to one another or intermarry. Napoleon constructing a galaxy of generals and courtiers, and even of monarchs, out of his collection of social nobodies; Julius Cæsar appointing as governor of Egypt the son of a freedman who but a short time before would have been legally disqualified for the post even of a private soldier in the Roman army; Louis XI making his barber his privy councillor: all these had in their different ways a firm hold of the scientific fact of human equality, expressed by Barbara in the Christian formula that all men are children of one father. No use declaring that all men are born free if we deny that they are born good. Guarantee a man's goodness and his liberty will take care of itself. To guarantee his freedom on condition that we approve of his moral character is formally to abolish all freedom whatsoever, as every man's liberty is at the mercy of moral indictments which any bigot can trump up against everyone who violates custom, whether as a prophet or as a rascal. This is the lesson Democracy has to learn before it can become anything but the most oppressive of all the priesthoods.

Let us now return to Bill Walker and his case of conscience against the Salvation Army. Major Barbara, not being a modern Tetzel, or the treasurer of a hospital, refuses to sell absolution to Bill for a pound sterling. Unfortunately, what the Army can afford to refuse to Bill Walker, it cannot refuse to Bodger. Bodger is master of the situation because he holds the purse strings. "Strive as you will" says Bodger, in effect: "me you cannot do without. You cannot save Bill Walker without my money." And the Army answers, quite rightly under the circumstances, "We will take money from the devil himself sooner than abandon the work of Salvation." So Bodger pays his conscience-money and gets the absolution that is refused to Bill. In real life Bill would perhaps never know this. But I, the dramatist whose business it is to shew the connexion between things that seem apart and unrelated in the haphazard order of events in real life, have contrived to make it known to Bill, with the result that the Salvation Army loses its hold of him at once.

But Bill may not be lost, for all that. He is still in the grip of the facts and of his own conscience, and may find his taste for blackguardism permanently spoiled. Still, I cannot guarantee that happy ending. Walk through the poorer quarters of our cities on Sunday when the men are not working, but resting and chewing the cud of their reflections. You will find one expression common to every mature face: the expression of cynicism. The discovery made by Bill Walker about the Salvation Army has been made by everyone there. They have found that every man has his price; and they have been foolishly or corruptly taught to mistrust and despise him for that necessary and salutary condition of social existence. When they learn that General Booth, too, has his price, they do not admire him because it is a high one, and admit the need of organizing society so that he shall get it in an honorable way: they conclude that his character is unsound and that all religious men are hypocrites and allies of their sweaters and oppressors. They know that the large subscriptions which help to support the Army are endowments, not of religion, but of the wicked doctrine of docility in poverty and humility under oppression; and they are rent by the most agonizing of all the doubts of the soul, the doubt whether their true salvation must not come from their most abhorrent passions, from murder, envy, greed, stubbornness, rage, and terrorism, rather than from public spirit, reasonableness, humanity, generosity, tenderness, delicacy, pity and kindness. The confirmation of that doubt, at which our newspapers have been working so hard for years past, is the morality of militarism; and the justification of militarism is that circumstances may at any time make it the true morality of the moment. This, which I wrote before 1914, has been most bloodily confirmed by two world wars.

At such moments it becomes the duty of the Churches to rally their congregations against the existing order. But if they do this, the existing order must forcibly suppress them. Churches are suffered to exist only on condition that they preach submission to the State as at present capitalistically organized. The Church of England itself is compelled to add to the thirtysix articles in which it formulates its religious tenets, three more in which it apologetically protests that the moment any of these articles comes in conflict with the State it is to be entirely renounced, abjured, violated, abrogated and abhorred, the policeman being a much more important person than any of the Persons of the Trinity. And this is why no tolerated Church nor Salvation Army can ever win the entire confidence of the poor. It must be on the side of the police and the military, no matter what it believes or disbelieves; and as the police and the military are the instruments by which the rich rob and oppress the poor (on legal and moral principles made for the purpose), it is not possible to be on the side of the poor and of the police at the same time. Indeed the religious bodies, as the almoners of the rich, become a sort of auxiliary police, taking off the insurrectionary edge of poverty with coals and blankets, bread and treacle, soothing and cheering the victims with hopes of immense and inexpensive happiness in another world when the process of working them to premature death in the service of the rich is complete in this.

Christianity and Anarchism

Such is the false position from which neither the Salvation Army nor the Church of England nor any other religious organization whatever can escape except through a reconstitution of society. Nor can they merely endure the State passively, washing their hands of its sins. The State is constantly forcing the consciences of men by violence and cruelty. Not content with exacting money from us for the maintenance of its soldiers and policemen, its gaolers and executioners, it forces us to take an active personal part in its proceedings on pain of becoming ourselves the victims of its violence. As I wrote these lines forty years ago a sensational example was given to the world. A royal marriage had been celebrated, first by sacrament in a cathedral, and then by a bullfight having for its main amusement the spectacle of horses gored and disembowelled by the bull, after which, when the bull was so exhausted as to be no longer dangerous, he was killed by a cautious matador. But the ironic contrast between the bullfight and the sacrament of marriage does not move anyone. Another contrast—that between the splendor, the happiness, the atmosphere of kindly admiration surrounding the young couple, and the price paid for it under our abominable social arrangements in the misery, squalor and degradation of millions of other young couples—was drawn at the same moment by an American novelist, Mr Upton Sinclair, who chipped a corner of the veneering from the huge meat packing industries of Chicago, and shewed it to us as a sample of what is going on all over the world underneath the top layer of prosperous plutocracy. One man was sufficiently moved by that contrast to pay his own life as the price of one terrible blow at the responsible parties. His poverty left him ignorant enough to be duped by the pretence that the innocent young bride and bridegroom, put forth and crowned by plutocracy as the heads of a State in which they had less personal power than any policeman, and less influence than any Chairman of a Trust, were responsible. At them accordingly he launched his sixpennorth of fulminate, missing his mark, but scattering the bowels of as many horses as any bull in the arena, and slaying twentythree persons, besides wounding ninetynine. And of all these, the horses alone were innocent of the guilt he was avenging: had he blown all Madrid to atoms with every adult person in it, not one could have escaped the charge of being an accessory, before, at, and after the facts, to poverty and prostitution, to such wholesale massacre of infants as Herod never dreamt of, to plague, pestilence and famine, battle, murder and lingering death: perhaps not one who had not helped, through example, precept, connivance, and even clamor, to teach the dynamiter his well-learnt gospel of hatred and vengeance, by approving every day of sentences of years of imprisonment so infernal in their unnatural stupidity and panic-stricken cruelty, that their advocates can disavow neither the dagger nor the bomb without stripping the mask of justice and humanity from themselves also.

At that very moment there appeared the biography of one of our dukes, who, being a Scot, could argue about politics, and therefore stood out as a great brain among our aristocrats. And what, if you please, was his Grace's favorite historical episode, which he declared he never read without intense satisfaction? Why, the young General

Bonaparte's pounding of the Paris mob to pieces in 1795, called in playful approval by our respectable classes " the whiff of grapeshot," though Napoleon, to do him justice, took a deeper view of it, and would fain have had it forgotten. And since the Duke was not a demon, but a man of like passions with ourselves, by no means rancorous or cruel as men go, who can doubt that all over the world proletarians of the ducal kidney revelled in " the whiff of dynamite " (the flavor of the joke seems to evaporate a little, does it not ?) because it was aimed at the class they hate even as our argute duke hated what he called the mob ?

In such an atmosphere there could be only one sequel to the Madrid explosion. All Europe burned to emulate it. Vengeance ! More blood ! Tear " the Anarchist beast " to shreds. Drag him to the scaffold. Imprison him for life. Let all civilized States band together to drive his like off the face of the earth ; and if any State refuses to join, make war on it. This time the leading London newspaper, then anti-Liberal and therefore anti-Tsarist in politics, did not say " Serve you right " to the victims, as it did, in effect, when Bobrikoff, and De Plehve, and Grand Duke Sergius, were in the same manner unofficially fulminated into fragments. No : fulminate our rivals in Asia by all means, ye brave Russian revolutionaries ; but to aim at an English princess ! monstrous ! hideous ! hound down the wretch to his doom ; and observe, please, that we are a civilized and merciful people, and, however much we may regret it, must not treat him as Ravaillac, Damiens, and our regicides of 1649 were treated.

Strangely enough, in the midst of this raging fire of malice, the one man who still had faith in the kindness and intelligence of human nature was the fulminator, a hunted wretch, with nothing, apparently, to secure his triumph over all the prisons and scaffolds of infuriate Europe except the revolver in his pocket and his readiness to discharge it at a moment's notice into his own head. Think of him setting out to find a gentleman and a Christian in the multitude of human wolves howling for his blood. Think also of this: that at the very first essay he found what he sought: a veritable grandee of Spain, a noble, high-thinking, unterrified, malice-void soul, in the guise—of all masquerades in the world!—of a modern editor. The Anarchist wolf, flying from the wolves of plutocracy, threw himself on the honor of the man. The man, not being a wolf (nor a London editor), and therefore not having enough sympathy with his exploit to be made bloodthirsty by it, did not throw him back to the pursuing wolves—gave him, instead, what help he could to escape, and sent him off acquainted at last with a force that goes deeper than dynamite, though you cannot buy so much of it for sixpence. That righteous and honorable high human deed was not wasted on Europe, let us hope, though it benefited the fugitive wolf for a moment only. The plutocratic wolves presently smelt him out. The fugitive shot the unlucky wolf whose nose was nearest; shot himself; and then convinced the world, by his photograph, that he was no monstrous freak of reversion to the tiger, but a good looking young man with nothing abnormal about him except his appalling courage and resolution (that is why the terrified shrieked Coward at him): one to whom murdering a happy young couple on their wedding morning would have been an unthinkably unnatural abomination under rational and kindly human circumstances.

Then comes the climax of irony and blind stupidity. The wolves, balked of their meal of fellow-wolf, turn on the Samaritan man, and proceed to torture him, after their manner, by imprisonment, for refusing to fasten his teeth in the throat of the dynamiter and hold him down until they came to finish him.

Thus, you see, a man may not be a gentleman nowadays even if he wishes to. As to being a Christian, he is allowed some latitude in that matter, because, I repeat, Christianity has two faces. Popular Christianity has for its emblem a gibbet; for its chief sensation a sanguinary execution after torture; for its central mystery an insane vengeance bought off by a trumpery expiation. But there is a nobler and profounder Christianity which affirms the sacred mystery of Equality, and forbids the glaring futility and folly of vengeance, often politely called punishment or justice. The gibbet part of Christianity is tolerated. The other is criminal felony. Connoisseurs in irony are well aware of the fact that the only editor in England who denounced punishment as radically wrong, also repudiated Christianity ; called his paper The Freethinker ; and was imprisoned for a year for " bad taste " under the law against blasphemy.

Sane Conclusions

And now I must ask the excited reader not to lose his head on one side or the other, but to draw a sane moral from these grim absurdities. It is not good sense to propose that laws against crime should apply to principals only and not to accessories whose consent, counsel, or silence may secure impunity to the principal. If you institute punishment as part of the law, you must punish people for refusing to punish. If you have a police, part of its duty must be to compel everybody to assist the police. No doubt if your laws are unjust, and your policemen agents of oppression, the result will be an unbearable violation of the private consciences of citizens. But that cannot be helped : the remedy is, not to license everybody to thwart the law if they please, but to make laws that will command the public assent, and not to deal cruelly and stupidly with law-breakers. Everybody disapproves of burglars ; but the modern burglar, when caught and overpowered by a householder, sometimes appeals, often, let us hope, with success, to his captor not to deliver him over to the useless horrors of penal servitude. In other cases the lawbreaker escapes because those who could give him up do not consider his breach of the law a guilty action. Private tribunals are formed in opposition to the official tribunals ; and these private tribunals employ assassins as executioners, as was done, for example, by Mahomet before he had established his power officially, and by the Ribbon lodges of Ireland in their long struggle with the landlords. Under such circumstances, the assassin goes free although everybody in men, when they are rascals, will not risk their skins for the good of humanity, and, when they are not, are sympathetic enough to care for humanity, abhorring murder, and never committing it until their consciences are outraged beyond endurance. The remedy is, then, simply not to outrage their consciences.

Do not be afraid that they will not make allowances. All men make very large allowances indeed before they stake their own lives in a war to the death with society. Nobody demands or expects the millennium. But there are two things that must be set right, or we shall perish, like Rome, of soul atrophy disguised as empire.

The first is, that the daily ceremony of dividing the wealth of the country among its inhabitants shall be so conducted that no crumb shall, save as a criminal's ration, go to any able-bodied adults who are not producing by their personal exertions not only a full equivalent for what they take, but a surplus sufficient to provide for their superannuation and pay back the debt due for their nurture.

The second is that the deliberate infliction of malicious injuries which now goes on under the name of punishment be abandoned ; so that the thief, the ruffian, the gambler, and the beggar, may without inhumanity be handed over to the law, and made to understand that a State which is too humane to punish will also be too thrifty to waste the life of honest men in watching or restraining dishonest ones. That is why we do not imprison dogs. We even take our chance of their first bite. But if a dog delights to bark and bite, it goes to the lethal chamber. That seems to me sensible. To allow the dog to expiate his bite by a period of torment, and then let him loose in a much more savage condition (for the chain makes a dog savage) to bite again and expiate again, having meanwhile spent a great deal of human life and happiness in the task of chaining and feeding and tormenting him, seems to me idiotic and superstitious. Yet that is what we do to men who bark and bite and steal. It would be far more sensible to put up with their vices, as we put up with their illnesses, until they give more trouble than they are worth, at which point we should, with many apologies and expressions of sympathy, and some generosity in complying with their last wishes, place them in the lethal chamber and get rid of them. Under no circumstances should they be allowed to expiate their misdeeds by a manufactured penalty, to subscribe to a charity, or to compensate the victims. If there is to be no punishment there can be no forgiveness. We shall never have real moral responsibility until everyone knows that his deeds are irrevocable, and that his life depends on his usefulness. Hitherto, alas! humanity has never dared face these hard facts. We frantically scatter conscience money and invent systems of conscience banking, with expiatory penalties, atonements, redemptions, salvations, hospital subscription lists and what not, to enable us to contract-out of the moral code. Not content with the old scapegoat and sacrificial lamb, we deify human saviors, and pray to miraculous virgin intercessors. We attribute mercy to the inexorable; soothe our consciences after committing murder by throwing ourselves on the bosom of divine love; and shrink even from our own gallows because we are forced to admit that it, at least, is irrevocable—as if one hour of imprisonment were not as irrevocable as any execution!

If a man cannot look evil in the face without illusion, he will never know what it really is, or combat it effectually. The few men who have been able (relatively) to do this have been called cynics, and have sometimes had an abnormal share of evil in themselves, corresponding to the abnormal strength of their minds; but they have never done mischief unless they intended to do it. That is why great scoundrels have been beneficent rulers whilst amiable and privately harmless monarchs have ruined their countries by trusting to the hocus-pocus of innocence and guilt, reward and punishment, virtuous indignation and pardon, instead of standing up to the facts without either malice or mercy. Major Barbara stands up to Bill Walker in that way, with the result that the ruffian who cannot get hated, has to hate himself. To relieve this agony he tries to get punished; but the Salvationist whom he tries to provoke is as merciless as Barbara, and only prays for him. Then he tries to pay, but can get nobody to take his money. His doom is the doom of Cain, who, failing to find either a savior, a policeman, or an almoner to help him to pretend that his brother's blood no longer cried from the ground, had to live and die a murderer. Cain took care not to commit another murder, unlike our railway shareholders (I am one) who kill and maim shunters by hundreds to save the cost of automatic couplings, and make atonement by annual subscriptions to deserving charities. Had Cain been allowed to pay off his score, he might possibly have killed Adam and Eve for the mere sake of a second luxurious reconciliation with God afterwards. Bodger, you may depend on it, will go on to the end of his life poisoning people with whisky, because he can always depend on the Salvation Army or the Church of England to negotiate a redemption for him in consideration of a trifling percentage of his profits.

There is a third condition too, which must be fulfilled before the great teachers of the world will cease to scoff at its religions. Creeds must become intellectually honest. At present there is not a single credible established religion in the world. That is perhaps the most stupendous fact in the whole world-situation. This play of mine, Major Barbara, is, I hope, both true and inspired ; but whoever says that it all happened, and that faith in it and understanding of it consist in believing that it is a record of an actual occurrence, is, to speak according to Scripture, a fool and a liar, and is hereby solemnly denounced and cursed as such by me, the author, to all posterity.

London, June 1906

Revised, April 1944,
in Ayot Saint Lawrence

PROLOGUE

Sunday morning in an open space at the East End of London. Bitter winter weather. A placard seven feet high stands beside an empty packing case upside down, with a reading desk in front of it: the two forming a tribune for a speaker. With this equipment a desperately small meeting is being addressed, or rather read to, by a young university don in spectacles, very smart in a new overcoat and spotless muffler, supported by a few undergraduates, male and female, very cold, and all trying not to look dispirited by their failure to attract the public, which consists of one policeman on duty and three or four East End workers waiting for the public houses to open, and deciding very doubtfully that the lecture to which they are listening is better than no entertainment at all. The scene is extremely depressing.

The placard is inscribed in the largest letters, UNIVERSITY EXTENSION OPEN AIR MEETINGS. UNDER THE AUSPICES OF THE WORKERS' EDUCATION ASSOCIATION. FIVE STAGES OF GREEK RELIGION. LECTURER ADOLPHUS CUSINS D.C.L., LITT.D., REGIUS PROFESSOR OF GREEK IN THE UNIVERSITY OF OXFORD. ALL SUNDAY MORNINGS IN FEBRUARY.

CUSINS [*reading with very distinct articulation but not looking at his audience*] The ancient Greeks considered it unseemly to give public praise to women for their good looks, but apparently thought it did no harm to young men. Note that, unlike our own popular playwrights in England and the United States, the great Athenians scorned what we call love interest and regarded sex appeal as indecent.

A BYSTANDER. S'truth ! [*He shrugs his shoulders and moves off*].

CUSINS. Listen to the words put into the mouth of Aeschylus by Aristophanes. He boasts of how he made the Greeks crave

Like lions to dash at the face of the foe, and leap to the call of the trumpet.

But no Sthenoboia I have given you, no : no Phaedra, no heroine strumpet.

If I have once put a woman in love in one act of one play may my teaching be scouted—

He is interrupted by the strains of a Salvation Army band playing a brisk march. Instantly the three remaining East Enders brighten up and hurry away in the direction of the sound.

CUSINS [*giving up in despair and thrusting his MS into his pocket*] No use. [*He descends from his platform and addresses himself to the police officer while his friends pack up the tribune and dismount the placard*] I am afraid this open air experiment is no good. Or else I havnt the knack of attracting an audience. If it hadnt been for you I expect they would have stoned me. I am afraid I must have bored you terribly.

POLICEMAN [*civil and respectful*] Oh no, sir : no no. Only it sounded a bit heathenish at first, almost as if you believed in them queer old gods : I talked to my missus about it. You see, sir, she's keen on the Salvation Army, and likes good serious talk. But when you said that morning that God was there all along, whatever they called him, I knew it was all right.

CUSINS. I never thought much of myself as a speaker ; but I have never lost my whole audience before.

POLICEMAN. Not at all, sir : I have heard worse. But there are two things that no speaker can stand up against.

CUSINS. And what are they, may I ask ?

POLICEMAN. One is a band : the other is a fight. The Salvation Army knows that : it always has a band. And this Sunday theres a special attraction. Theres Major Barbara.

CUSINS. Major Barbara ! How can a woman be a major ?

POLICEMAN. She can, sir, in the army, or a sergeant, or a colonel, or even a general. If you want a tip or two as to how to gather a meeting and hold it you might do worse than follow that band to the Salvation Barracks and hear her take the Sunday service.

CUSINS. Egad, I will. I have a fancy for collecting religious experiences. Which way?

POLICEMAN. Come with me, sir. I'm off duty now that your meeting is over.

They go off together to the exterior of the Salvation Barracks. The meeting inside is overflowing into the doorway, which is crowded.

CUSINS. It's full up. We cant get in.

POLICEMAN. I can, sir. Keep close behind me. [*He pushes into the crowd*]. Now then: by your leave. This gentleman is on business. By your leave.

They push through to the interior of the hall. Room is made for them silently at the end of one of the forms. Barbara is on the platform speaking. Whilst she speaks Cusins' face shews that he is fascinated and keenly interested by Barbara herself, though not, like the rest, by what she is saying.

BARBARA. Amid all the poverty and ugliness of our lives here, the sin and the suffering, the grime and the smoke, the toil and the struggle, you know, and I know, that God is with us always and everywhere. We do not need a cathedral to worship Him in. Here in this old shed no less than beneath God's open sky we can draw nearer to Him. Some of you feel Him near you even now, and feel, too, how much you need Him. Wont you let Him come into your life now, today, as so many have done before? You want His strength, His guidance, His comfort: you need His forgiveness and friendship. Some of you turn away from Him in bitterness at the hardship of your lives, saying that you do not want God: you want happiness and beauty. God will give you both. There is no beauty like the beauty of the newly saved who has found the unspeakable happiness that only the consciousness of God's presence and love can give. We in the Army have our daily trials. Most of us are as poor as you are. But we are all happy; and the mark of that happiness is on us for you to see. The rich are not happy. The poor have only to reach out their hands for God's happiness and take it. Is there anyone here who has courage enough to raise his hand as a sign that he would like us to pray for him? Make the decision now: in your need and loneliness God is waiting for you. Someone here must feel that he should raise his hand, but that it isnt easy. It is the easiest thing in the world: he has often done it to beckon to his child or to stop a tram. He feels too shy perhaps. Never mind: I will pray for him; and God will give him the courage of a lion. Come: do not keep God waiting: thousands have done it; and if you can find me one who has done it and been sorry afterwards I will put off this dear uniform and never pray again. Come come! I know there is someone. [*Scanning their faces along the row her look meets that of Cusins. His hand shoots up instantly*]. Ah! I have found him. Let the brave gentleman come to the front: make room for him, please. [*Cusins passes up, all staring at him*]. Give me your hand, my brother. I will take you to our little room for confession where we will pray together. Friends: you will sing "How sweet the name of Jesus sounds!"

They rise and sing while she leads Cusins out through a side door into a small cloakroom, with overcoats hanging up and a table heaped with women's outdoor belongings. Along the table is a form, the only sitting accommodation in the place. Barbara sits and places Cusins beside her.

BARBARA. Now before we pray a little together, may I tell you to forget that we have never met before. You must not be shy and distant with me. I can see that all's well with you. I can see in your face the new happiness that has just come into your life. You are a new man: you are saved. You feel that, dont you?

CUSINS [*grimly determined*] Listen to me, Major Barbara. I am here on false pretences. It is true that a new happiness has come into my life: a happiness that I have never quite believed in—that at any rate I thought would never come into my life. It has come.

BARBARA. Thank God!

CUSINS. Take care. It has not made me a better man: it has made me an utterly unscrupulous one.

BARBARA. What do you mean?

CUSINS. Look at me. Look deep into my eyes. Is the new happiness that you see there the kind of happiness you are thinking of?

BARBARA [*looking hard*] It must be. There is no other happiness like it. It gladdens my heart because, under God, I have brought it there.

CUSINS. Good. Now let me warn you that though I am a scholar and a gentleman I am as poor as a church mouse, like all scholars. I am no good for anything in the way of worldly success.

BARBARA. Oh, what does that matter? We are all poor here. We never think of money or success. When all our money is spent on the Army we pray for more; and it comes: it always comes. Take your mind off such things. And now, shall we pray together?

CUSINS. I never pray—at least not in your way. The new thing that has come to me is not that I am saved. I was saved when I was five years old, when I first swallowed your religion. Since then I have swallowed twenty religions: that is my life's work. I know all their catchwords. They are nothing to me: I am interested in the essence of all religions, not in their catchwords or in yours.

BARBARA. Let us find it for you here. We can.

CUSINS. Nonsense! I have more to teach you about religion than you can yet imagine.

BARBARA. You think so. Then why have you come here with me? Why did you hold up your hand?

CUSINS. Because I have impulses that I cannot explain. They come very seldom. But when they come, nothing can stop me. There is an end of my conscience, of my prudence, of my reason. Such an impulse seized me the moment I saw you. You are poor; you are ignorant; our table manners are different; our relatives will not mix; everything is against our associating with oneanother. No matter: to be with you I will join the Army: I will put on the uniform and beat the drum: in short, I am hopelessly and for ever in love with you and will follow you to the end of the world until you marry me. Is that plain?

BARBARA [*rising, calm and greatly amused*] Perfectly. And now will you begin by seeing me home? I should like to put you through your first trial by shewing you where I live and introducing you to my family.

CUSINS. I do not care where you live; and I will face ten families for you.

BARBARA [*putting on her cloak and gathering her bag*] So you shall. God has some little surprises for you, my friend. Come.

They go out by a door which leads to an alley beside the building, where they can sidetrack the crowd.

CUSINS. Have we far to go? What about a taxi?

BARBARA. We dont run to taxis in this part of the world. Most of us here have never been in one. We must walk to a tram.

They go off accordingly to a tram-stop in a main east end thoroughfare.

BARBARA. Here we are. Look out for a number 23.

CUSINS. But we are on the wrong side, are we not? This is the side for the trams going west.

BARBARA. We are going west.

CUSINS. Oh, I beg pardon. Where do you live?

BARBARA. In a place called Wilton Crescent.

CUSINS. Quite a fashionable address. I did not know that there is a Wilton Crescent at the east end. The only one I know is at Hyde Park Corner close to Belgrave Square. Where all the dukes and earls live. Have you ever been as far west as Hyde Park Corner?

BARBARA. Occasionally. I know the Wilton Crescent you mean. I live there.

CUSINS. But—but—but—

BARBARA. Why not? Plenty of poor people live there. How do you know that I am not a scullery maid? Here is number 23. [*She runs to the tram-car to secure a seat*]. Jump in.

They get into the car. It drives off ; and in due course they arrive on the doorstep of the house in Wilton Crescent.

CUSINS. I ring the servants' bell, I suppose. Had I not better leave you before they open ?

BARBARA. Dont ring. I have a latchkey. [*She produces it*].

CUSINS. By the way, I had better know your name before I go in.

BARBARA. You have not mentioned yours. And it is I who have to introduce you.

CUSINS. My name is Adolphus Cusins.

BARBARA. Adolphus ! What a name ! I shall call you Dolly.

CUSINS. My relatives do. I wish they didnt. Introduce me as Professor Cusins.

BARBARA. Allude to me as Miss Undershaft.

CUSINS [*thunderstruck*] Undershaft ! ! ! The Cannon King ! The rival of Krupp and of Skoda ! The multi-millionaire ! !

BARBARA. Do not faint, Dolly. I have not seen him since I was that high [*indicating a height of about three feet*]. You will find my mother, Lady Britomart Undershaft, much more terrifying. [*She unlocks the door and goes in*].

CUSINS. So this is one of the little surprises you promised ! Heaven help me ! [*He goes in ; and the door closes behind them*].

So ends the prologue. The story begins some weeks later in her boudoir upstairs, where Lady Britomart Undershaft sits at her writing table after dinner. A large and comfortable settee is in the middle of the room with a copy of The Speaker, a Liberal weekly journal, on it. A person sitting on it (it is vacant at present) would have, on his right, the writing table, with the lady herself busy at it ; the heavily curtained windows on his left with a smaller writing-table and an armchair near them ; the door behind him towards his right ; and additional sitting accommodation for half a dozen persons.

Lady Britomart is a mature governing class aristocrat, well dressed and yet careless of her dress, well bred and quite reckless of her breeding, well mannered and yet appallingly outspoken and indifferent to the opinion of her interlocutors, amiable and yet peremptory, arbitrary, and high-tempered to the last bearable degree, and withal a very typical managing matron of the upper class, treated as a naughty child until she grew into a scolding mother, and finally settling down with plenty of practical ability and worldly experience, limited in the oddest way with domestic and class limitations, conceiving the universe exactly as if it were a large house in Wilton Crescent, though handling her corner of it very effectively on that assumption, and being quite enlightened and liberal as to the books in the library, the pictures on the walls, the music in the portfolios, and the articles in the papers.

Her son Stephen comes in. He is a gravely correct young man, taking himself very seriously, and, though still in some awe of his mother from childish habit and bachelor shyness, quite untroubled by doubts or diffidence.

STEPHEN. Whats the matter?

LADY BRITOMART. Presently, Stephen.

Stephen submissively walks to the settee and sits down. He takes The Speaker.

LADY BRITOMART. Dont begin to read, Stephen. I shall require all your attention.

STEPHEN. It was only while I was waiting—

LADY BRITOMART. Dont make excuses, Stephen. [*He puts down The Speaker*]. Now! [*She finishes her writing; rises; and comes to the settee*]. I have not kept you waiting very long, I think.

STEPHEN. Not at all, mother.

LADY BRITOMART. Bring me my cushion. [*He takes the cushion from the chair at the desk and arranges it for her as she sits down on the settee*]. Sit down. [*He sits down and fingers his tie nervously*]. Dont fiddle with your tie, Stephen: there is nothing the matter with it.

STEPHEN. I beg your pardon. [*He fiddles with his watch chain instead*].

LADY BRITOMART. Now are you attending to me, Stephen?

STEPHEN. Of course, mother.

LADY BRITOMART. No: it's n o t of course. I want something much more than your everyday matter-of-course attention. I am going to speak to you very seriously, Stephen. I wish you would let that chain alone.

STEPHEN [*hastily relinquishing the chain*] Have I done anything to annoy you, mother? If so, it was quite unintentional.

LADY BRITOMART [*astonished*] Nonsense! [*With some remorse*] My poor boy, did you think I was angry with you?

STEPHEN. What is it, then, mother? You are making me very uneasy.

LADY BRITOMART [*squaring herself at him rather aggressively*] Stephen: may I ask how soon you intend to realize that you are a grown-up man, and that I am only a woman?

STEPHEN [*amazed*] Only a—

LADY BRITOMART. Dont repeat my words, please: it is a most aggravating habit. You must learn to face life seriously, Stephen. I really cannot bear the whole burden of our family affairs any longer. You must advise me: you must assume the responsibility.

STEPHEN. I!

LADY BRITOMART. Yes, you, of course. You were twenty-four last June. Youve been at Harrow and Cambridge. Youve been to India and Japan. You must know a lot of things, now; unless you have wasted your time most scandalously. Well, a d v i s e me.

STEPHEN [*much perplexed*] You know I have never interfered in the household—

LADY BRITOMART. No: I should think not. I dont want you to order the dinner.

STEPHEN. I mean in our family affairs.

LADY BRITOMART. Well, you must interfere now; for they are getting quite beyond me.

STEPHEN [*troubled*] I have thought sometimes that perhaps I ought; but really, mother, I know so little about them; and what I do know is so painful! it is so impossible to mention some things to you— [*he stops, ashamed*].

LADY BRITOMART. I suppose you mean your father.

STEPHEN [*almost inaudibly*] Yes.

LADY BRITOMART. My dear : we cant go on all our lives not mentioning him. Of course you were quite right not to open the subject until I asked you to ; but you are old enough now to be taken into my confidence, and to help me to deal with him about the girls.

STEPHEN. But the girls are all right. They are engaged.

LADY BRITOMART [*complacently*] Yes : I have made a very good match for Sarah. Charles Lomax will be a millionaire when he is thirty-five. But in the meantime his trustees cannot under the terms of his father's will allow him more than £800 a year.

STEPHEN. But the will says also that if he increases his income by his own exertions, they may double the increase.

LADY BRITOMART. Charles Lomax's exertions are much more likely to decrease his income than to increase it. Sarah will have to find at least another £800 a year for the next ten years ; and even then they will be as poor as church mice. And what about Barbara ? I thought Barbara was going to make the most brilliant career of all of you. And what does she do ? Joins the Salvation Army ; discharges her maid ; lives on a pound a week ; and walks in one evening with a professor of Greek whom she has picked up in the street, and who pretends to be a Salvationist, and actually plays the big drum for her in public because he has fallen head over ears in love with her.

STEPHEN. I was certainly rather taken aback when I heard they were engaged. Cusins is a very nice fellow, certainly : nobody would ever guess that he was born in Australia ; but—

LADY BRITOMART. Oh, Adolphus Cusins will make a very good husband. After all, nobody can say a word against Greek : it stamps a man at once as an educated gentleman. And my family, thank Heaven, is not a pig-headed Tory one. We are Whigs, and believe in liberty. Let snobbish people say what they please: Barbara shall marry, not the man they like, but the man *I* like.

STEPHEN. Of course I was thinking only of his income. However, he is not likely to be extravagant.

LADY BRITOMART. Dont be too sure of that, Stephen. I know your quiet, simple, refined, poetic people like Adolphus: quite content with the best of everything! They cost more than your extravagant people, who are always as mean as they are second rate. No: Barbara will need at least £2000 a year. You see it means two additional households. Besides, my dear, *you* must marry soon. I dont approve of the present fashion of philandering bachelors and late marriages; and I am trying to arrange something for you.

STEPHEN. It's very good of you, mother; but perhaps I had better arrange that for myself.

LADY BRITOMART. Nonsense! you are much too young to begin matchmaking: you would be taken in by some pretty little nobody. Of course I dont mean that you are not to be consulted: you know that as well as I do. [*Stephen closes his lips and is silent*]. Now dont sulk, Stephen.

STEPHEN. I am not sulking, mother. What has all this got to do with—with—with my father?

LADY BRITOMART. My dear Stephen: where is the money to come from? It is easy enough for you and the other children to live on my income as long as we are in the same house; but I cant keep four families in four separate houses. You know how poor my father is: he has barely seven thousand a year now; and really, if he were not the Earl of Stevenage, he would have to give up society. He can do nothing for us. He says, naturally enough, that it is absurd that he should be asked to provide for the children of a man who is rolling in money. You see, Stephen, your father must be fabulously wealthy, because there is always a war going on somewhere.

STEPHEN. You need not remind me of that, mother. I have hardly ever opened a newspaper in my life without seeing our name in it. The Undershaft torpedo! The Undershaft quick firers! The Undershaft ten inch! the Undershaft disappearing rampart gun! the Undershaft submarine! and now the Undershaft aerial battleship! At Harrow they called me the Woolwich Infant. At Cambridge it was the same. A little brute at King's who was always trying to get up revivals, spoilt my Bible—your first birthday present to me—by writing under my name, "Son and heir to Undershaft and Lazarus, Death and Destruction Dealers: address, Christendom and Judea." But that was not so bad as the way I was kowtowed to everywhere because my father was making millions by selling cannons.

LADY BRITOMART. It is not only the cannons, but the war loans that Lazarus arranges under cover of giving credit for the cannons. You know, Stephen, it's perfectly scandalous. Those two men, Andrew Undershaft and Lazarus, positively have Europe under their thumbs. That is why your father is able to behave as he does. He is above the law. Do you think Bismarck or Gladstone or Disraeli could have openly defied every social and moral obligation all their lives as your father has? They simply wouldnt have dared. I asked Gladstone to take it up. I asked The Times to take it up. I asked the Lord Chamberlain to take it up. But it was just like asking them to declare war on the Sultan. They wouldnt. They said they couldnt touch him. I believe they were afraid.

STEPHEN. What could they do? He does not actually break the law.

LADY BRITOMART. Not break the law! He is always breaking the law. He broke the law when he was born: his parents were not married.

STEPHEN. Mother! Is that true?

LADY BRITOMART. Of course it's true: that was why we separated.

STEPHEN. He married without letting you know this!

LADY BRITOMART [*rather taken aback by this inference*] Oh no. To do Andrew justice, that was not the sort of thing he did. Besides, you know the Undershaft motto: Unashamed. Everybody knew.

STEPHEN. But you said that was why you separated.

LADY BRITOMART. Yes, because he was not content with being a foundling himself: he wanted to disinherit you for another foundling. That was what I couldnt stand.

STEPHEN [*ashamed*] Do you mean for—for—for—

LADY BRITOMART. Dont stammer, Stephen. Speak distinctly.

STEPHEN. But this is so frightful to me, mother. To have to speak to you about such things!

LADY BRITOMART. It's not pleasant for me, either, especially if you are still so childish that you must make it worse by a display of embarrassment. It is only in the middle classes, Stephen, that people get into a state of dumb helpless horror when they find that there are wicked people in the world. In our class, we have to decide what is to be done with wicked people; and nothing should disturb our self-possession. Now ask your question properly.

STEPHEN. Mother: have you no consideration for me? For Heaven's sake either treat me as a child, as you always do, and tell me nothing at all; or tell me everything and let me take it as best I can.

LADY BRITOMART. Treat you as a child! What do you mean? It is most unkind and ungrateful of you to say such a thing. You know I have never treated any of you as children. I have always made you my companions and friends, and allowed you perfect freedom to do and say whatever you liked, so long as you liked what I could approve of.

STEPHEN [*desperately*] I daresay we have been the very imperfect children of a very perfect mother; but I do beg you to let me alone for once, and tell me about this horrible business of my father wanting to set me aside for another son.

LADY BRITOMART [*amazed*] Another son! I never said anything of the kind. I never dreamt of such a thing. This is what comes of interrupting me.

STEPHEN. But you said—

LADY BRITOMART [*cutting him short*] Now be a good boy, Stephen, and listen to me patiently. The Undershafts are descended from a foundling in the parish of St Andrew Undershaft in the city. That was long ago, in the reign of James the First. Well, this foundling was adopted by an armorer and gun-maker. In the course of time the foundling succeeded to the business ; and from some notion of gratitude, or some vow or something, he adopted another foundling, and left the business to him. And that foundling did the same. Ever since that, the cannon business has always been left to an adopted foundling named Andrew Undershaft.

STEPHEN. But did they never marry ? Were there no legitimate sons ?

LADY BRITOMART. Oh yes : they married just as your father did ; and they were rich enough to buy land for their own children and leave them well provided for. But they always adopted and trained some foundling to succeed them in the business ; and of course they always quarrelled with their wives furiously over it. Your father was adopted in that way ; and he pretends to consider himself bound to keep up the tradition and adopt somebody to leave the business to. Of course I was not going to stand that. There may have been some reason for it when the Undershafts could only marry women in their own class, whose sons were not fit to govern great estates. But there could be no excuse for passing over my son.

STEPHEN [*dubiously*] I am afraid I should make a poor hand of managing a cannon foundry.

LADY BRITOMART. Nonsense ! you could easily get a manager and pay him a salary.

STEPHEN. My father evidently had no great opinion of my capacity.

LADY BRITOMART. Stuff, child ! you were only a baby : it had nothing to do with your capacity. Andrew did it on principle, just as he did every perverse and wicked thing on principle. When my father remonstrated, Andrew actually told him to his face that history tells us of only two successful institutions: one the Undershaft firm, and the other the Roman Empire under the Antonines. That was because the Antonine emperors all adopted their successors. Such rubbish! The Stevenages are as good as the Antonines, I hope; and you are a Stevenage. But that was Andrew all over. There you have the man! Always clever and unanswerable when he was defending nonsense and wickedness: always awkward and sullen when he had to behave sensibly and decently!

STEPHEN. Then it was on my account that your home life was broken up, mother. I am sorry.

LADY BRITOMART. Well, dear, there were other differences. I really cannot bear an immoral man. I am not a Pharisee, I hope; and I should not have minded his merely doing wrong things: we are none of us perfect. But your father didnt exactly do wrong things: he said them and thought them: that was what was so dreadful. He really had a sort of religion of wrongness. Just as one doesnt mind men practising immorality so long as they own that they are in the wrong by preaching morality; so I couldnt forgive Andrew for preaching immorality while he practised morality. You would all have grown up without principles, without any knowledge of right and wrong, if he had been in the house. You know, my dear, your father was a very attractive man in some ways. Children did not dislike him; and he took advantage of it to put the wickedest ideas into their heads, and make them quite unmanageable. I did not dislike him myself: very far from it; but nothing can bridge over moral disagreement.

STEPHEN. All this simply bewilders me, mother. People may differ about matters of opinion, or even about religion; but how can they differ about right and wrong? Right is right; and wrong is wrong; and if a man cannot distinguish them properly, he is either a fool or a rascal: thats all.

LADY BRITOMART [*touched*] Thats my own boy [*she pats his cheek*]! Your father never could answer that: he used to laugh and get out of it under cover of some affectionate nonsense. And now that you understand the situation, what do you advise me to do?

STEPHEN. Well, what can you do?

LADY BRITOMART. I must get the money somehow.

STEPHEN. We cannot take money from him. I had rather go and live in some cheap place like Bedford Square or even Hampstead than take a farthing of his money.

LADY BRITOMART. But after all, Stephen, our present income comes from Andrew.

STEPHEN [*shocked*] I never knew that.

LADY BRITOMART. Well, you surely didnt suppose your grandfather had anything to give me. The Stevenages could not do everything for you. We gave you social position. Andrew had to contribute something. He had a very good bargain, I think.

STEPHEN [*bitterly*] We are utterly dependent on him and his cannons, then?

LADY BRITOMART. Certainly not: the money is settled. But he provided it. So you see it is not a question of taking money from him or not: it is simply a question of how much. I dont want any more for myself.

STEPHEN. Nor do I.

LADY BRITOMART. But Sarah does; and Barbara does. That is, Charles Lomax and Adolphus Cusins will cost them more. So I must put my pride in my pocket and ask for it, I suppose. That is your advice, Stephen, is it not?

STEPHEN. No.

LADY BRITOMART [*sharply*] Stephen!

STEPHEN. Of course if you are determined—

LADY BRITOMART. I am not determined: I ask your advice; and I am waiting for it. I will not have all the responsibility thrown on my shoulders.

STEPHEN [*obstinately*] I would die sooner than ask him for another penny.

LADY BRITOMART [*resignedly*] You mean that *I* must ask him. Very well, Stephen: it shall be as you wish. You will be glad to know that your grandfather concurs. But he thinks I ought to ask Andrew to come here and see the girls. After all, he must have some natural affection for them.

STEPHEN. Ask him here ! ! !

LADY BRITOMART. Do not repeat my words, Stephen. Where else can I ask him ?

STEPHEN. I never expected you to ask him at all.

LADY BRITOMART. Now dont tease, Stephen. Come ! you see that it is necessary that he should pay us a visit, dont you ?

STEPHEN [*reluctantly*] I suppose so, if the girls cannot do without his money.

LADY BRITOMART. Thank you, Stephen: I knew you would give me the right advice when it was properly explained to you. I have asked your father to come this evening. [*Stephen bounds from his seat*] Dont jump, Stephen: it fidgets me.

STEPHEN [*in utter consternation*] Do you mean to say that my father is coming here tonight—that he may be here at any moment ?

LADY BRITOMART [*looking at her watch*] I said nine. [*He gasps. She rises*]. Ring the bell, please. [*Stephen goes to the smaller writing table: presses a button on it; and sits at it with his elbows on the table and his head in his hands, outwitted and overwhelmed*]. It is ten minutes to nine yet; and I have to prepare the girls. I asked Charles Lomax and Adolphus to dinner on purpose that they might be here. Andrew had better see them in case he should cherish any delusions as to their being capable of supporting their wives. [*The butler enters: Lady Britomart goes behind the settee to speak to him*]. Morrison: go up to the drawing room and tell everybody to come down here at once. [*Morrison withdraws. Lady Britomart turns to Stephen*]. Now remember, Stephen: I shall need all your countenance and authority. [*He rises and tries to recover some vestige of these attributes*]. Give me a chair, dear. [*He pushes a chair forward from the wall to where she stands, near the smaller writing table. She sits down ; and he goes to the armchair, into which he throws himself*]. I dont know how Barbara will take it. Ever since they made her a major in the Salvation Army she has developed a propensity to have her own way and order people about which quite cows me sometimes. It's not ladylike : I'm sure I dont know where she picked it up. Anyhow, Barbara shant bully me ; but still it's just as well that your father should be here before she has time to refuse to meet him or make a fuss. Dont look nervous, Stephen : it will only encourage Barbara to make difficulties. *I* am nervous enough, goodness knows ; but I dont shew it.

Sarah and Barbara come in with their respective young men, Charles Lomax and Adolphus Cusins. Sarah is slender, bored, and mundane. Barbara is robuster, jollier, much more energetic. Sarah is fashionably dressed : Barbara is in Salvation Army uniform. Lomax, a young man about town, is like many other young men about town. He is afflicted with a frivolous sense of humor which plunges him at the most inopportune moments into paroxysms of imperfectly suppressed laughter. Cusins is a spectacled student, slight, thin haired, and sweet voiced, with a more complex form of Lomax's complaint. His sense of humor is intellectual and subtle, and is complicated by an appalling temper. The lifelong struggle of a benevolent temperament and a high conscience against impulses of inhuman ridicule and fierce impatience has set up a chronic strain which has visibly wrecked his constitution. He is a most implacable, determined, tenacious, intolerant person who by mere force of character presents himself as—and indeed actually is—considerate, gentle, explanatory, even mild and apologetic, capable possibly of murder, but not of cruelty or coarseness. By the operation of some instinct which is not merciful enough to blind him with the illusions of love, he is obstinately bent on marrying Barbara. Lomax likes

Sarah and thinks it will be rather a lark to marry her. Consequently he has not attempted to resist Lady Britomart's arrangements to that end.

All four look as if they had been having a good deal of fun in the drawing room. The girls enter first, leaving the swains outside. Sarah comes to the settee. Barbara comes in after her and stops at the door.

BARBARA. Are Cholly and Dolly to come in?

LADY BRITOMART [*forcibly*] Barbara: I will not have Charles called Cholly: the vulgarity of it positively makes me ill.

BARBARA. It's all right, mother: Cholly is quite correct nowadays. Are they to come in?

LADY BRITOMART. Yes, if they will behave themselves.

BARBARA [*through the door*] Come in, Dolly; and behave yourself.

Barbara comes to her mother's writing table. Cusins enters smiling, and wanders towards Lady Britomart.

SARAH [*calling*] Come in, Cholly. [*Lomax enters, controlling his features very imperfectly, and places himself vaguely between Sarah and Barbara*].

LADY BRITOMART [*peremptorily*] Sit down, all of you. [*They sit. Cusins crosses to the window and seats himself there. Lomax takes a chair. Barbara sits at the writing table and Sarah on the settee*]. I dont in the least know what you are laughing at, Adolphus. I am surprised at you, though I expected nothing better from Charles Lomax.

CUSINS [*in a remarkably gentle voice*] Barbara has been trying to teach me the West Ham Salvation March.

LADY BRITOMART. I see nothing to laugh at in that; nor should you if you are really converted.

CUSINS [*sweetly*] You were not present. It was really funny, I believe.

LOMAX. Ripping.

LADY BRITOMART. Be quiet, Charles. Now listen to me, children. Your father is coming here this evening.

General stupefaction. Lomax, Sarah, and Barbara rise: Sarah scared, and Barbara amused and expectant.

LOMAX [*remonstrating*] Oh I say!

LADY BRITOMART. You are not called on to say anything, Charles.

SARAH. Are you serious, mother?

LADY BRITOMART. Of course I am serious. It is on your account, Sarah, and also on Charles's. [*Silence. Sarah sits, with a shrug. Charles looks painfully unworthy*]. I hope you are not going to object, Barbara.

BARBARA. I! why should I? My father has a soul to be saved like anybody else. He's quite welcome as far as I am concerned. [*She sits on the table, and softly whistles 'Onward, Christian Soldiers'*].

LOMAX [*still remonstrant*] But really, dont you know! Oh I say!

LADY BRITOMART [*frigidly*] What do you wish to convey, Charles?

LOMAX. Well, you must admit that this is a bit thick.

LADY BRITOMART [*turning with ominous suavity to Cusins*] Adolphus: you are a professor of Greek. Can you translate Charles Lomax's remarks into reputable English for us?

CUSINS [*cautiously*] If I may say so, Lady Brit, I think Charles has rather happily expressed what we all feel. Homer, speaking of Autolycus, uses the same phrase; πυκινὸν δόμον ἐλθεῖν means a bit thick.

LOMAX [*handsomely*] Not that I mind, you know, if Sarah dont. [*He sits*].

LADY BRITOMART [*crushingly*] Thank you. Have I *your* permission, Adolphus, to invite my own husband to my own house?

CUSINS [*gallantly*] You have my unhesitating support in everything you do.

LADY BRITOMART. Tush! Sarah: have you nothing to say?

SARAH. Do you mean that he is coming regularly to live here?

LADY BRITOMART. Certainly not. The spare room is ready for him if he likes to stay for a day or two and see a little more of you; but there are limits.

SARAH. Well, he cant eat us, I suppose. *I* dont mind.

LOMAX [*chuckling*] I wonder how the old man will take it.

LADY BRITOMART. Much as the old woman will, no doubt, Charles.

LOMAX [*abashed*] I didnt mean—at least—

LADY BRITOMART. You didnt think, Charles. You never do ; and the result is, you never mean anything. And now please attend to me, children. Your father will be quite a stranger to us.

LOMAX. I suppose he hasnt seen Sarah since she was a little kid.

LADY BRITOMART. Not since she was a little kid, Charles, as you express it with that elegance of diction and refinement of thought that seem never to desert you. Accordingly—er— [*impatiently*] Now I have forgotten what I was going to say. That comes of your provoking me to be sarcastic, Charles. Adolphus : will you kindly tell me where I was.

CUSINS [*sweetly*] You were saying that as Mr Undershaft has not seen his children since they were babies, he will form his opinion of the way you have brought them up from their behavior tonight, and that therefore you wish us all to be particularly careful to conduct ourselves well, especially Charles.

LADY BRITOMART [*with emphatic approval*] Precisely.

LOMAX. Look here, Dolly : Lady Brit didnt say that.

LADY BRITOMART [*vehemently*] I did, Charles. Adolphus's recollection is perfectly correct. It is most important that you should be good ; and I do beg you for once not to pair off into opposite corners and giggle and whisper while I am speaking to your father.

BARBARA. All right, mother. We'll do you credit. [*She comes off the table, and sits in her chair with ladylike elegance*].

LADY BRITOMART. Remember, Charles, that Sarah will want to feel proud of you instead of ashamed of you.

LOMAX. Oh I say ! theres nothing to be exactly proud of, dont you know.

LADY BRITOMART. Well, try and look as if there was.

Morrison, pale and dismayed, breaks into the room in unconcealed disorder.

MORRISON. Might I speak a word to you, my lady?

LADY BRITOMART. Nonsense! Shew him up.

MORRISON. Yes, my lady. [*He goes*].

LOMAX. Does Morrison know who it is?

LADY BRITOMART. Of course. Morrison has always been with us.

LOMAX. It must be a regular corker for him, dont you know.

LADY BRITOMART. Is this a moment to get on my nerves, Charles, with your outrageous expressions?

LOMAX. But this is something out of the ordinary, really—

MORRISON [*at the door*] The—er—Mr Undershaft. [*He retreats in confusion*].

Andrew Undershaft comes in. All rise. Lady Britomart meets him in the middle of the room behind the settee.

Andrew is, on the surface, a stoutish, easygoing elderly man, with kindly patient manners, and an engaging simplicity of character. But he has a watchful, deliberate, waiting, listening face, and formidable reserves of power, both bodily and mental, in his capacious chest and long head. His gentleness is partly that of a strong man who has learnt by experience that his natural grip hurts ordinary people unless he handles them very carefully, and partly the mellowness of age and success. He is also a little shy in his present very delicate situation.

LADY BRITOMART. Good evening, Andrew.

UNDERSHAFT. How d'ye do, my dear.

LADY BRITOMART. You look a good deal older.

UNDERSHAFT [*apologetically*] I am somewhat older. [*Taking her hand with a touch of courtship*] Time has stood still with you.

LADY BRITOMART [*throwing away his hand*] Rubbish! This is your family.

UNDERSHAFT [*surprised*] Is it so large? I am sorry to say my memory is failing very badly in some things. [*He offers his hand with paternal kindness to Lomax*].

LOMAX [*jerkily shaking his hand*] Ahdedoo.

UNDERSHAFT. I can see you are my eldest. I am very glad to meet you again, my boy.

LOMAX [*remonstrating*] No, but look here dont you know—[*Overcome*] Oh I say!

LADY BRITOMART [*recovering from momentary speechlessness*] Andrew: do you mean to say that you dont remember how many children you have?

UNDERSHAFT. Well, I am afraid I—. They have grown so much—er. Am I making any ridiculous mistake? I may as well confess: I recollect only one son. But so many things have happened since, of course—er—

LADY BRITOMART [*decisively*] Andrew: you are talking nonsense. Of course you have only one son.

UNDERSHAFT. Perhaps you will be good enough to introduce me, my dear.

LADY BRITOMART. That is Charles Lomax, who is engaged to Sarah.

UNDERSHAFT. My dear sir, I beg your pardon.

LOMAX. Notatall. Delighted, I assure you.

LADY BRITOMART. This is Stephen.

UNDERSHAFT [*bowing*] Happy to make your acquaintance, Mr Stephen. Then [*going to Cusins*] you must be my son. [*Taking Cusins' hands in his*] How are you, my young friend? [*To Lady Britomart*] He is very like you, my love.

CUSINS. You flatter me, Mr Undershaft. My name is Cusins: engaged to Barbara. [*Very explicitly*] That is Major Barbara Undershaft, of the Salvation Army. That is Sarah, your second daughter. This is Stephen Undershaft, your son.

UNDERSHAFT. My dear Stephen, I beg your pardon.

STEPHEN. Not at all.

UNDERSHAFT. Mr Cusins: I am much indebted to you for explaining so precisely. [*Turning to Sarah*] Barbara, my dear—

SARAH [*prompting him*] Sarah.

UNDERSHAFT. Sarah, of course. [*They shake hands. He goes over to Barbara*] Barbara—I am right this time, I hope?

BARBARA. Quite right. [*They shake hands*].

LADY BRITOMART [*resuming command*] Sit down, all of you.

Sit down, Andrew. [*She comes forward and sits on the settee. Cusins also brings his chair forward on her left. Barbara and Stephen resume their seats. Lomax gives his chair to Sarah and goes for another*].

UNDERSHAFT. Thank you, my love.

LOMAX [*conversationally, as he brings a chair forward between the writing table and the settee, and offers it to Undershaft*] Takes you some time to find out exactly where you are, dont it?

UNDERSHAFT [*accepting the chair, but remaining standing*] That is not what embarrasses me, Mr Lomax. My difficulty is that if I play the part of a father, I shall produce the effect of an intrusive stranger; and if I play the part of a discreet stranger, I may appear a callous father.

LADY BRITOMART. There is no need for you to play any part at all, Andrew. You had much better be sincere and natural.

UNDERSHAFT [*submissively*] Yes, my dear: I daresay that will be best. [*He sits down comfortably*]. Well, here I am. Now what can I do for you all?

LADY BRITOMART. You need not do anything, Andrew. You are one of the family. You can sit with us and enjoy yourself.

A painfully conscious pause. Barbara makes a face at Lomax, whose too long suppressed mirth immediately explodes in agonized neighings.

LADY BRITOMART [*outraged*] Charles Lomax: if you can behave yourself, behave yourself. If not, leave the room.

LOMAX. I'm awfully sorry, Lady Brit; but really you know, upon my soul! [*He sits on the settee between Lady Britomart and Undershaft, quite overcome*].

BARBARA. Why dont you laugh if you want to, Cholly? It's good for your inside.

LADY BRITOMART. Barbara: you have had the education of a lady. Please let your father see that; and dont talk like a street girl.

UNDERSHAFT. Never mind me, my dear. As you know, I am not a gentleman; and I was never educated.

LOMAX [*encouragingly*] Nobody'd know it, I assure you. You look all right, you know.

CUSINS. Let me advise you to study Greek, Mr Undershaft. Greek scholars are privileged men. Few of them know Greek; and none of them know anything else; but their position is unchallengeable. Other languages are the qualifications of waiters and commercial travellers: Greek is to a man of position what the hallmark is to silver.

BARBARA. Dolly: dont be insincere. Cholly: fetch your concertina and play something for us.

LOMAX [*jumps up eagerly, but checks himself to remark doubtfully to Undershaft*] Perhaps that sort of thing isnt in your line, eh?

UNDERSHAFT. I am particularly fond of music.

LOMAX [*delighted*] Are you? Then I'll get it. [*He goes upstairs for the instrument*].

UNDERSHAFT. Do you play, Barbara?

BARBARA. Only the tambourine. But Cholly's teaching me the concertina.

UNDERSHAFT. Is Cholly also a member of the Salvation Army?

BARBARA. No: he says it's bad form to be a dissenter. But I dont despair of Cholly. I made him come yesterday to a meeting at the dock gates, and take the collection in his hat.

UNDERSHAFT [*looks whimsically at his wife*] ! !

LADY BRITOMART. It is not my doing, Andrew. Barbara is old enough to take her own way. She has no father to advise her.

BARBARA. Oh yes she has. There are no orphans in the Salvation Army.

UNDERSHAFT. Your father there has a great many children and plenty of experience, eh?

BARBARA [*looking at him with quick interest and nodding*] Just so. How did you come to understand that? [*Lomax is heard at the door trying the concertina*].

LADY BRITOMART. Come in, Charles. Play us something at once.

LOMAX. Righto! [*He sits down in his former place, and preludes*].

UNDERSHAFT. One moment, Mr Lomax, I am rather interested in the Salvation Army. Its motto might be my own: Blood and Fire.

LOMAX [*shocked*] But not your sort of blood and fire, you know.

UNDERSHAFT. My sort of blood cleanses: my sort of fire purifies.

BARBARA. So do ours. Come down tomorrow to my shelter—the West Ham shelter—and see what we're doing. We're going to march to a great meeting in the Assembly Hall at Mile End. Come and see the shelter and then march with us: it will do you a lot of good. Can you play anything?

UNDERSHAFT. In my youth I earned pennies, and even shillings occasionally, in the streets and in public house parlors by my natural talent for stepdancing. Later on, I became a member of the Undershaft orchestral society, and performed passably on the tenor trombone.

LOMAX [*scandalized—putting down the concertina*] Oh I say!

BARBARA. Many a sinner has played himself into heaven on the trombone, thanks to the Army.

LOMAX [*to Barbara, still rather shocked*] Yes: but what about the cannon business, dont you know? [*To Undershaft*] Getting into heaven is not exactly in your line, is it?

LADY BRITOMART. Charles!!!

LOMAX. Well; but it stands to reason, dont it? The cannon business may be necessary and all that: we cant get on without cannons; but it isnt right, you know. On the other hand, there may be a certain amount of tosh about the Salvation Army—I belong to the Established Church myself—but still you cant deny that it's religion; and you cant go against religion, can you? At least unless youre downright immoral, dont you know.

UNDERSHAFT. You hardly appreciate my position, Mr Lomax—

LOMAX [*hastily*] I'm not saying anything against you personally—

UNDERSHAFT. Quite so, quite so. But consider for a moment. Here I am, a profiteer in mutilation and murder. I find myself in a specially amiable humor just now because, this morning, down at the foundry, we blew twenty-seven dummy soldiers into fragments with a gun which formerly destroyed only thirteen.

LOMAX [*leniently*] Well, the more destructive war becomes, the sooner it will be abolished, eh?

UNDERSHAFT. Not at all. The more destructive war becomes the more fascinating we find it. No, Mr Lomax: I am obliged to you for making the usual excuse for my trade; but I am not ashamed of it. I am not one of those men who keep their morals and their business in water-tight compartments. All the spare money my trade rivals spend on hospitals, cathedrals, and other receptacles for conscience money, I devote to experiments and researches in improved methods of destroying life and property. I have always done so; and I always shall. Therefore your Christmas card moralities of peace on earth and goodwill among men are of no use to me. Your Christianity, which enjoins you to resist not evil, and to turn the other cheek, would make me a bankrupt. My morality—my religion—must have a place for cannons and torpedoes in it.

STEPHEN [*coldly—almost sullenly*] You speak as if there were half a dozen moralities and religions to choose from, instead of one true morality and one true religion.

UNDERSHAFT. For me there is only one true morality; but it might not fit you, as you do not manufacture aerial battleships. There is only one true morality for every man; but every man has not the same true morality.

LOMAX [*overtaxed*] Would you mind saying that again? I didnt quite follow it.

CUSINS. It's quite simple. As Euripides says, one man's meat is another man's poison morally as well as physically.

UNDERSHAFT. Precisely.

LOMAX. Oh, *that*! Yes, yes, yes. True. True.

STEPHEN. In other words, some men are honest and some are scoundrels.

BARBARA. Bosh! There are no scoundrels.

UNDERSHAFT. Indeed? Are there any good men?

BARBARA. No. Not one. There are neither good men nor scoundrels: there are just children of one Father; and the sooner they stop calling one another names the better. You neednt talk to me: I know them. Ive had scores of them through my hands: scoundrels, criminals, infidels, philanthropists, missionaries, county councillors, all sorts. Theyre all just the same sort of sinner; and theres the same salvation ready for them all.

UNDERSHAFT. May I ask have you ever saved a maker of cannons?

BARBARA. No. Will you let me try?

UNDERSHAFT. Well, I will make a bargain with you. If I go to see you tomorrow in your Salvation Shelter, will you come the day after to see me in my cannon works?

BARBARA. Take care. It may end in your giving up the cannons for the sake of the Salvation Army.

UNDERSHAFT. Are you sure it will not end in your giving up the Salvation Army for the sake of the cannons?

BARBARA. I will take my chance of that.

UNDERSHAFT. And I will take my chance of the other. [*They shake hands on it*]. Where is your shelter?

BARBARA. In West Ham. At the sign of the cross. Ask anybody in Canning Town. Where are your works?

UNDERSHAFT. In Perivale St Andrews. At the sign of the sword. Ask anybody in Europe.

LOMAX. Hadnt I better play something?

BARBARA. Yes. Give us 'Onward, Christian Soldiers.'

LOMAX. Well, thats rather a strong order to begin with, dont you know. Suppose I sing Thourt passing hence, my brother. It's much the same tune.

BARBARA. It's too melancholy. You get saved, Cholly; and youll pass hence, my brother, without making such a fuss about it.

LADY BRITOMART. Really, Barbara, you go on as if religion were a pleasant subject. Do have some sense of propriety.

UNDERSHAFT. I do not find it an unpleasant subject, my dear. It is the only one that capable people really care for.

LADY BRITOMART [*looking at her watch*] Well, if you are determined to have it, I insist on having it in a proper and respectable way. Charles : ring for prayers.

General amazement. Stephen rises in dismay.

LOMAX [*rising*] Oh I say !

UNDERSHAFT [*rising*] I am afraid I must be going.

LADY BRITOMART. You cannot go now, Andrew : it would be most improper. Sit down. What will the servants think ?

UNDERSHAFT. My dear : I have conscientious scruples. May I suggest a compromise ? If Barbara will conduct a little service in the drawing room, with Mr Lomax as organist, I will attend it willingly. I will even take part, if a trombone can be procured.

LADY BRITOMART. Dont mock, Andrew.

UNDERSHAFT [*shocked—to Barbara*] You dont think I am mocking, my love, I hope.

BARBARA. No, of course not ; and it wouldnt matter if you were : half the Army came to their first meeting for a lark. [*Rising*] Come along. [*She throws her arm round her father and sweeps him out, calling to the others from the threshold*] Come, Dolly. Come, Cholly.

Cusins rises.

LADY BRITOMART. I will not be disobeyed by everybody. Adolphus : sit down. [*He does not*]. Charles : you may go. You are not fit for prayers : you cannot keep your countenance.

LOMAX. Oh I say ! [*He goes out*].

LADY BRITOMART [*continuing*] But you, Adolphus, can behave yourself if you choose to. I insist on your staying.

CUSINS. My dear Lady Brit : there are things in the family prayer book that I couldnt bear to hear you say.

LADY BRITOMART. What things, pray ?

CUSINS. Well, you would have to say before all the servants

that we have done things we ought not to have done, and left undone things we ought to have done, and that there is no health in us. I cannot bear to hear you doing yourself such an injustice, and Barbara such an injustice. As for myself, I flatly deny it : I have done my best. I shouldnt dare to marry Barbara—I couldnt look you in the face—if it were true. So I must go to the drawing room.

LADY BRITOMART [*offended*] Well, go. [*He starts for the door*]. And remember this, Adolphus [*he turns to listen*] : I have a very strong suspicion that you went to the Salvation Army to worship Barbara and nothing else. And I quite appreciate the very clever way in which you systematically humbug me. I have found you out. Take care Barbara doesnt. Thats all.

CUSINS [*with unruffled sweetness*] Dont tell on me. [*He steals out*].

LADY BRITOMART. Sarah : if you want to go, go. Anything's better than to sit there as if you wished you were a thousand miles away.

SARAH [*languidly*] Very well, mamma. [*She goes*].

Lady Britomart, with a sudden flounce, gives way to a little gust of tears.

STEPHEN [*going to her*] Mother : whats the matter ?

LADY BRITOMART [*swishing away her tears with her handkerchief*] Nothing. Foolishness. You can go with him, too, if you like, and leave me with the servants.

STEPHEN. Oh, you mustnt think that, mother. I—I dont like him.

LADY BRITOMART. The others do. That is the injustice of a woman's lot. A woman has to bring up her children ; and that means to restrain them, to deny them things they want, to set them tasks, to punish them when they do wrong, to do all the unpleasant things. And then the father, who has nothing to do but pet them and spoil them, comes in when all her work is done and steals their affection from her.

STEPHEN. He has not stolen our affection from you. It is only curiosity.

LADY BRITOMART [*violently*] I wont be consoled, Stephen. There is nothing the matter with me. [*She rises and goes towards the door*].

STEPHEN. Where are you going, mother?

LADY BRITOMART. To the drawing room, of course. [*She goes out. 'Onward, Christian Soldiers,' on the concertina, with tambourine accompaniment, is heard when the door opens*]. Are you coming, Stephen?

STEPHEN. No. Certainly not. [*She goes. He sits down on the settee, with compressed lips and an expression of strong dislike*].

The yard of the West Ham shelter of the Salvation Army is a cold place on a January morning. The building itself, an old warehouse, is newly whitewashed. Its gabled end projects into the yard in the middle, with a door on the ground floor, and another in the loft above it without any balcony or ladder, but with a pulley rigged over it for hoisting sacks. Those who come from this central gable end into the yard have the gateway leading to the street on their left, with a stone horse-trough just beyond it, and, on the right, a penthouse shielding a table from the weather. There are forms at the table ; and on them are seated a man and a woman, both much down on their luck, finishing a meal of bread (one thick slice each, with margarine and golden syrup) and diluted milk.

The man, a workman out of employment, is young, agile, a talker, a poser, sharp enough to be capable of anything in reason except honesty or altruistic considerations of any kind. The woman is a commonplace old bundle of poverty and hard-worn humanity. She looks sixty and probably is forty-five. If they were rich people, gloved and muffed and well wrapped up in furs and overcoats, they would be numbed and miserable ; for it is a grindingly cold raw January day ; and a glance at the background of grimy warehouses and leaden sky visible over the whitewashed walls of the yard would drive any idle rich person straight to the Mediterranean. But these two, being no more troubled with visions of the Mediterranean than of the moon, and being compelled to keep more of their clothes in the pawnshop, and less on their persons, in winter than in summer, are not depressed by the cold: rather are they stung into vivacity, to which their meal has just now given an almost jolly turn. The man takes a pull at his mug, and then gets up and moves about the yard with his hands deep in his pockets, occasionally breaking into a stepdance.

THE WOMAN. Feel better arter your meal, sir?

THE MAN. No. Call that a meal! Good enough for you, praps; but wot is it to me, an intelligent workin man.

THE WOMAN. Workin man! Wot are you?

THE MAN. Painter.

THE WOMAN [*sceptically*] Yus, I dessay.

THE MAN. Yus, you dessay! I know. Every loafer that cant do nothink calls isself a painter. Well, I'm a real painter: grainer, finisher, thirty-eight bob a week when I can get it.

THE WOMAN. Then why dont you go and get it?

THE MAN. I'll tell you why. Fust: I'm intelligent—fffff! it's rotten cold here [*he dances a step or two*]—yes: intelligent beyond the station o life into which it has pleased the capitalists to call me; and they dont like a man that sees through em. Second, an intelligent bein needs a doo share of appiness; so I drink somethink cruel when I get the chawnce. Third, I stand by my class and do as little as I can so's to leave arf the job for me fellow workers. Fourth, I'm fly enough to know wots inside the law and wots outside it; and inside it I do as the capitalists do: pinch wot I can lay me ands on. In a proper state of society I am sober, industrious and honest: in Rome, so to speak, I do as the Romans do. Wots the consequence? When trade is bad—and it's rotten bad just now—and the employers az to sack arf their men, they generally start on me.

THE WOMAN. Whats your name?

THE MAN. Price. Bronterre O'Brien Price. Usually called Snobby Price, for short.

THE WOMAN. Snobby's a carpenter, aint it? You said you was a painter.

PRICE. Not that kind of snob, but the genteel sort. I'm too uppish, owing to my intelligence, and my father being a Chartist and a reading, thinking man : a stationer, too. I'm none of your common hewers of wood and drawers of water ; and dont you forget it. [*He returns to his seat at the table, and takes up his mug*]. Wots your name ?

THE WOMAN. Rummy Mitchens, sir.

PRICE [*quaffing the remains of his milk to her*] Your elth, Miss Mitchens.

RUMMY [*correcting him*] Missis Mitchens.

PRICE. Wot ! Oh Rummy, Rummy ! Respectable married woman, Rummy, gittin rescued by the Salvation Army by pretendin to be a bad un. Same old game !

RUMMY. What am I to do ? I cant starve. Them Salvation lasses is dear good girls ; but the better you are, the worse they likes to think you were before they rescued you. Why shouldnt they av a bit o credit, poor loves ? theyre worn to rags by their work. And where would they get the money to rescue us if we was to let on we're no worse than other people ? You know what ladies and gentlemen are.

PRICE. Thievin swine ! Wish I ad their job, Rummy, all the same. Wot does Rummy stand for ? Pet name praps ?

RUMMY. Short for Romola.

PRICE. For wot ! ?

RUMMY. Romola. It was out of a new book. Somebody me mother wanted me to grow up like.

PRICE. We're companions in misfortune, Rummy. Both on us got names that nobody cawnt pronounce. Consequently I'm Snobby and youre Rummy because Bill and Sally wasnt good enough for our parents. Such is life !

RUMMY. Who saved you, Mr Price ? Was it Major Barbara?

PRICE. No : I come here on my own. I'm going to be Bronterre O'Brien Price, the converted painter. I know wot they like. I'll tell em how I blasphemed an gambled and wopped my poor old mother—

RUMMY [*shocked*] Used you to beat your mother?

PRICE. Not likely. She used to beat me. No matter: you come and listen to the converted painter, and youll hear how she was a pious woman that taught me me prayers at er knee, an how I used to come home drunk and drag her out o bed be er snow white airs, an lam into er with the poker.

RUMMY. Thats whats so unfair to us women. Your confessions is just as big lies as ours: you dont tell what you really done no more than us; but you men can tell your lies right out at the meetins and be made much of for it; while the sort o confessions we az to make az to be wispered to one lady at a time. It aint right, spite of all their piety.

PRICE. Right! Do you spose the Army 'd be allowed if it went and did right? Not much. It combs our air and makes us good little blokes to be robbed and put upon. But I'll play the game as good as any of em. I'll see somebody struck by lightnin, or hear a voice sayin "Snobby Price: where will you spend eternity?" I'll av a time of it, I tell you.

RUMMY. You wont be let drink, though.

PRICE. I'll take it out in gorspellin, then. I dont want to drink if I can get fun enough any other way.

Jenny Hill, a pale, overwrought, pretty Salvation lass of eighteen, comes in through the yard gate, leading Peter Shirley, a half hardened, half worn-out elderly man, weak with hunger.

JENNY [*supporting him*] Come! pluck up. I'll get you something to eat. Youll be all right then.

PRICE [*rising and hurrying officiously to take the old man off Jenny's hands*] Poor old man! Cheer up, brother: youll find rest and peace and appiness ere. Hurry up with the food, miss: e's fair done. [*Jenny hurries into the shelter*]. Ere, buck up, daddy! she's fetchin y'a thick slice o breadn treacle, an a mug o skyblue. [*He seats him at the corner of the table*].

RUMMY [*gaily*] Keep up your old art! Never say die!

SHIRLEY. I'm not an old man. I'm only forty-six. I'm as

good as ever I was. The grey patch come in my hair before I was thirty. All it wants is three pennorth o hair dye: am I to be turned on the streets to starve for it? Holy God! I've worked ten to twelve hours a day since I was thirteen, and paid my way all through; and now am I to be thrown into the gutter and my job given to a young man that can do it no better than me because Ive black hair that goes white at the first change?

PRICE [*cheerfully*] No good jawrin about it. Youre ony a jumped-up, jerked-off, orspittle-turned-out incurable of an ole workin man: who cares about you? Eh? Make the thievin swine give you a meal: theyve stole many a one from you. Get a bit o your own back. [*Jenny returns with the usual meal*]. There you are, brother. Awsk a blessin an tuck that into you.

SHIRLEY [*looking at it ravenously but not touching it, and crying like a child*] I never took anything before.

JENNY [*petting him*] Come, come! the Lord sends it to you: he wasnt above taking bread from his friends; and why should you be? Besides, when we find you a job you can pay us for it if you like.

SHIRLEY [*eagerly*] Yes, yes: thats true. I can pay you back: it's only a loan. [*Shivering*] Oh Lord! oh Lord! [*He turns to the table and attacks the meal ravenously*].

JENNY. Well, Rummy, are you more comfortable now?

RUMMY. God bless you, lovey! youve fed my body and saved my soul, havnt you? [*Jenny, touched, kisses her*]. Sit down and rest a bit: you must be ready to drop.

JENNY. Ive been going hard since morning. But theres more work than we can do. I mustnt stop.

RUMMY. Try a prayer for just two minutes. Youll work all the better after.

JENNY [*her eyes lighting up*] Oh isnt it wonderful how a few minutes prayer revives you! I was quite lightheaded at twelve o'clock, I was so tired; but Major Barbara just sent me to pray for five minutes; and I was able to go on as if I had only just begun. [*To Price*] Did you have a piece of bread?

PRICE [*with unction*] Yes, miss; but Ive got the piece that I value more ; and thats the peace that passeth hall hannerstennin.

RUMMY [*fervently*] Glory Hallelujah !

Bill Walker, a rough customer of about twenty-five, appears at the yard gate and looks malevolently at Jenny.

JENNY. That makes me so happy. When you say that, I feel wicked for loitering here. I must get to work again.

She is hurrying to the shelter, when the new-comer moves quickly up to the door and intercepts her. His manner is so threatening that she retreats as he comes at her truculently, driving her down the yard.

BILL. Aw knaow you. Youre the one that took awy maw girl. Youre the one that set er agen me. Well, I'm gowin to ev er aht. Not that Aw care a carse for er or you : see? Bat Aw'll let er knaow ; and Aw'll let you knaow. Aw'm gowin to give her a doin thatll teach er to cat awy from me. Nah in wiv you and tell er to cam aht afore Aw cam in and kick er aht. Tell er Bill Walker wants er. She'll knaow wot thet means ; and if she keeps me witin itll be worse. You stop to jawr beck at me ; and Aw'll stawt on you : d'ye eah? Theres your wy. In you gow. [*He takes her by the arm and slings her towards the door of the shelter. She falls on her hand and knee. Rummy helps her up again*].

PRICE [*rising, and venturing irresolutely towards Bill*] Easy there, mate. She aint doin you no arm.

BILL. Oo are you callin mite? [*Standing over him threateningly*] Youre gowin to stend ap for er, aw yer? Put ap your ands.

RUMMY [*running indignantly to him to scold him*] Oh, you great brute— [*He instantly swings his left hand back against her face. She screams and reels back to the trough, where she sits down, covering her bruised face with her hands and rocking herself and moaning with pain*].

JENNY [*going to her*] Oh, God forgive you ! How could you strike an old woman like that?

BILL [*seizing her by the hair so violently that she also screams, and tearing her away from the old woman*] You Gawd forgimme again an Aw'll Gawd forgive you one on the jawr thetll stop you pryin for a week. [*Holding her and turning fiercely on Price*] Ev you ennything to sy agen it?

PRICE [*intimidated*] No, matey: she aint anything to do with me.

BILL. Good job for you! Aw'd pat two meals into you and fawt you with one finger arter, you stawved cur. [*To Jenny*] Nah are you gowin to fetch aht Mog Ebbijem; or em Aw to knock your fice off you and fetch her meself?

JENNY [*writhing in his grasp*] Oh please someone go in and tell Major Barbara—[*she screams again as he wrenches her head down; and Price and Rummy flee into the shelter*].

BILL. You want to gow in and tell your Mijor of me, do you?

JENNY. Oh please dont drag my hair. Let me go.

BILL. Do you or downt you? [*She stifles a scream*]. Yus or nao?

JENNY. God give me strength—

BILL [*striking her with his fist in the face*] Gow an shaow her thet, and tell her if she wants one lawk it to cam and interfere with me. [*Jenny, crying with pain, goes into the shed. He goes to the form and addresses the old man*]. Eah: finish your mess; an git aht o maw wy.

SHIRLEY [*springing up and facing him fiercely, with the mug in his hand*] You take a liberty with me, and I'll smash you over the face with the mug and cut your eye out. Aint you satisfied—young whelps like you—with takin the bread out o the mouths of your elders that have brought you up and slaved for you, but you must come shovin and cheekin and bullyin in here, where the bread o charity is sickenin in our stummicks?

BILL [*contemptuously, but backing a little*] Wot good are you, you aold palsy mag? Wot good are you?

SHIRLEY. As good as you and better. I'll do a day's work agen you or any fat young soaker of your age. Go and take my job at Horrockses, where I worked for ten year. They want young men there: they cant afford to keep men over forty-five. Theyre very sorry—give you a character and happy to help you to get anything suited to your years—sure a steady man wont be long out of a job. Well, let em try *you*. Theyll find the differ. What do *you* know? Not as much as how to beeyave yourself—layin your dirty fist across the mouth of a respectable woman!

BILL. Downt provowk me to ly it acrost yours: d'ye eah?

SHIRLEY [*with blighting contempt*] Yes: you like an old man to hit, dont you, when youve finished with the women. I aint seen you hit a young one yet.

BILL [*stung*] You loy, you aold soupkitchener, you. There was a yang menn eah. Did Aw offer to itt him or did Aw not?

SHIRLEY. Was he starvin or was he not? Was he a man or only a crosseyed thief an a loafer? Would you hit my son-in-law's brother?

BILL. Oo's ee?

SHIRLEY. Todger Fairmile o Balls Pond. Him that won £20 off the Japanese wrastler at the music hall by standin out 17 minutes 4 seconds agen him.

BILL [*sullenly*] Aw'm nao music awl wrastler. Ken he box?

SHIRLEY. Yes: an you cant.

BILL. Wot! Aw cawnt, cawnt Aw? Wots thet you sy [*threatening him*]?

SHIRLEY [*not budging an inch*] Will you box Todger Fairmile if I put him on to you? Say the word.

BILL [*subsiding with a slouch*] Aw'll stend ap to enny menn alawv, if he was ten Todger Fairmawls. But Aw dont set ap to be a perfeshnal.

SHIRLEY [*looking down on him with unfathomable disdain*] *You* box! Slap an old woman with the back o your hand! You hadnt even the sense to hit her where a magistrate couldnt see the mark of it, you silly young lump of conceit and ignorance. Hit a girl in the jaw and ony make her cry! If Todger Fairmile'd done it, she wouldnt a got up inside o ten minutes, no more than you would if he got on to you. Yah! I'd set about you myself if I had a week's feedin in me instead o two months' starvation. [*He turns his back on him and sits down moodily at the table*].

BILL [*following him and stooping over him to drive the taunt in*] You loy ! youve the bread and treacle in you that you cam èah to beg.

SHIRLEY [*bursting into tears*] Oh God ! it's true ; I'm only an old pauper on the scrap heap. [*Furiously*] But youll come to it yourself ; and then youll know. Youll come to it sooner than a teetotaller like me, fillin yourself with gin at this hour o the mornin !

BILL. Aw'm nao gin drinker, you oald lawr ; bat wen Aw want to give my girl a bloomin good awdin Aw lawk to ev a bit o devil in me : see ? An cah Aw emm, talkin to a rotten aold blawter like you sted o givin her wot for. [*Working himself into a rage*] Aw'm gowin in there to fetch her aht. [*He makes vengefully for the shelter door*].

SHIRLEY. Youre goin to the station on a stretcher, more likely ; and theyll take the gin and the devil out of you there when they get you inside. You mind what youre about : the major here is the Earl o Stevenage's granddaughter.

BILL [*checked*] Garn !

SHIRLEY. Youll see.

BILL [*his resolution oozing*] Well, Aw aint dan nathin to er.

SHIRLEY. Spose she said you did ! who'd believe you ?

BILL [*very uneasy, skulking back to the corner of the penthouse*] Gawd ! theres no jastice in this cantry. To think wot them people can do ! Aw'm as good as er.

SHIRLEY. Tell her so. It's just what a fool like you would do.

Barbara, brisk and businesslike, comes from the shelter with a note book, and addresses herself to Shirley. Bill, cowed, sits down in the corner on a form, and turns his back on them.

BARBARA. Good morning.

SHIRLEY [*standing up and taking off his hat*] Good morning, miss.

BARBARA. Sit down : make yourself at home. [*He hesitates ;*

but she puts a friendly hand on his shoulder and makes him obey]. Now then! since youve made friends with us, we want to know all about you. Names and addresses and trades.

SHIRLEY. Peter Shirley. Fitter. Chucked out two months ago because I was too old.

BARBARA [*not at all surprised*] Youd pass still. Why didnt you dye your hair?

SHIRLEY. I did. Me age come out at a coroner's inquest on me daughter.

BARBARA. Steady?

SHIRLEY. Teetotaller. Never out of a job before. Good worker. And sent to the knackers like an old horse!

BARBARA. No matter: if you did your part God will do his.

SHIRLEY [*suddenly stubborn*] My religion's no concern of anybody but myself.

BARBARA [*guessing*] *I* know. Secularist?

SHIRLEY [*hotly*] Did I offer to deny it?

BARBARA. Why should you? My own father's a Secularist, I think. Our Father—yours and mine—fulfils himself in many ways; and I daresay he knew what he was about when he made a Secularist of you. So buck up, Peter! we can always find a job for a steady man like you. [*Shirley, disarmed and a little bewildered, touches his hat. She turns from him to Bill*]. Whats your name?

BILL [*insolently*] Wots thet to you?

BARBARA [*calmly making a note*] Afraid to give his name. Any trade?

BILL. Oo's afride to give is nime? [*Doggedly, with a sense of heroically defying the House of Lords in the person of Lord Stevenage*] If you want to bring a chawge agen me, bring it. [*She waits, unruffled*]. Moy nime's Bill Walker.

BARBARA [*as if the name were familiar: trying to remember how*] Bill Walker? [*Recollecting*] Oh, I know: youre the man that Jenny Hill was praying for inside just now. [*She enters his name in her note book*].

BILL. Oo's Jenny Ill? And wot call as she to pry for me?

BARBARA. I dont know. Perhaps it was you that cut her lip.

BILL [*defiantly*] Yus, it was me that cat her lip. Aw aint afride o you.

BARBARA. How could you be, since youre not afraid of God? Youre a brave man, Mr Walker. It takes some pluck to do our work here; but none of us dare lift our hand against a girl like that, for fear of her father in heaven.

BILL [*sullenly*] I want nan o your kentin jawr. I spowse you think Aw cam eah to beg from you, like this demmiged lot eah. Not me. Aw downt want your bread and scripe and ketlep. Aw dont blieve in your Gawd, no more than you do yourself.

BARBARA [*sunnily apologetic and ladylike, as on a new footing with him*] Oh, I beg your pardon for putting your name down, Mr Walker. I didnt understand. I'll strike it out.

BILL [*taking this as a slight, and deeply wounded by it*] Eah! you let maw nime alown. Aint it good enaff to be in your book?

BARBARA [*considering*] Well, you see, theres no use putting down your name unless I can do something for you, is there? Whats your trade?

BILL [*still smarting*] Thets nao concern o yours.

BARBARA. Just so. [*Very businesslike*] I'll put you down as [*writing*] the man who—struck—poor little Jenny Hill—in the mouth.

BILL [*rising threateningly*] See eah. Awve ed enaff o this.

BARBARA [*quite sunny and fearless*] What did you come to us for?

BILL. Aw cam for maw gel, see? Aw cam to tike her aht o this and to brike er jawr for er.

BARBARA [*complacently*] You see I was right about your trade. [*Bill, on the point of retorting furiously, finds himself, to his great shame and terror, in danger of crying instead. He sits down again suddenly*]. Whats her name?

BILL [*dogged*] Er nime's Mog Ebbijem: thets wot her nime is.

BARBARA. Mog Habbijam! Oh, she's gone to Canning Town, to our barracks there.

BILL [*fortified by his resentment of Mog's perfidy*] Is she? [*Vindictively*] Then Aw'm gowin to Kennintahn arter her. [*He crosses to the gate ; hesitates ; finally comes back at Barbara*]. Are you loyin to me to git shat o me?

BARBARA. I dont want to get shut of you. I want to keep you here and save your soul. Youd better stay : youre going to have a bad time today, Bill.

BILL. Oo's gowin to give it to me? You, preps?

BARBARA. Someone you dont believe in. But youll be glad afterwards.

BILL [*slinking off*] Aw'll gow to Kennintahn to be aht o reach o your tangue. [*Suddenly turning on her with intense malice*] And if Aw downt fawnd Mog there, Aw'll cam beck and do two years for you, selp me Gawd if Aw downt!

BARBARA [*a shade kindlier, if possible*] It's no use, Bill. She's got another bloke.

BILL. Wot!

BARBARA. One of her own converts. He fell in love with her when he saw her with her soul saved, and her face clean, and her hair washed.

BILL [*surprised*] Wottud she wash it for, the carroty slat? It's red.

BARBARA. It's quite lovely now, because she wears a new look in her eyes with it. It's a pity youre too late. The new bloke has put your nose out of joint, Bill.

BILL. Aw'll put his nowse aht o joint for him. Not that Aw care a carse for er, mawnd thet. But Aw'll teach her to drop me as if Aw was dirt. And Aw'll teach him to meddle with maw judy. Wots iz bleedin nime?

BARBARA. Sergeant Todger Fairmile.

SHIRLEY [*rising with grim joy*] I'll go with him, miss. I want to see them two meet. I'll take him to the infirmary when it's over.

BILL [*to Shirley, with undissembled misgiving*] Is thet im you was speakin on?

SHIRLEY. Thats him.

BILL. Im that wrastled in the music awl?

SHIRLEY. The competitions at the National Sportin Club was worth nigh a hundred a year to him. He's gev em up now for religion ; so he's a bit fresh for want of the exercise he was accustomed to. He'll be glad to see you. Come along.

BILL. Wots is wight ?

SHIRLEY. Thirteen four. [*Bill's last hope expires*].

BARBARA. Go and talk to him, Bill. He'll convert you.

SHIRLEY. He'll convert your head into a mashed potato.

BILL [*sullenly*] Aw aint afride of im. Aw aint afride of ennybody. Bat e can lick me. She's dan me. [*He sits down moodily on the edge of the horse trough*].

SHIRLEY. You aint goin. I thought not. [*He resumes his seat*].

BARBARA [*calling*] Jenny !

JENNY [*appearing at the shelter door with a plaster on the corner of her mouth*] Yes, Major.

BARBARA. Send Rummy Mitchens out to clear away here.

JENNY. I think she's afraid.

BARBARA [*her resemblance to her mother flashing out for a moment*] Nonsense ! she must do as she's told.

JENNY [*calling into the shelter*] Rummy : the Major says you must come.

Jenny comes to Barbara, purposely keeping on the side next Bill, lest he should suppose that she shrank from him or bore malice.

BARBARA. Poor little Jenny ! Are you tired ? [*Looking at the wounded cheek*] Does it hurt ?

JENNY. No : it's all right now. It was nothing.

BARBARA [*critically*] It was as hard as he could hit, I expect. Poor Bill ! You dont feel angry with him, do you ?

JENNY. Oh no, no, no : indeed I dont, Major, bless his poor heart ! [*Barbara kisses her ; and she runs away merrily into the shelter. Bill writhes with an agonizing return of his new and alarming symptoms, but says nothing. Rummy Mitchens comes from the shelter*].

BARBARA [*going to meet Rummy*] Now Rummy, bustle. Take in those mugs and plates to be washed ; and throw the crumbs about for the birds.

Rummy takes the three plates and mugs ; but Shirley takes back his mug from her, as there is still some milk left in it.

RUMMY. There aint any crumbs. This aint a time to waste good bread on birds.

PRICE [*appearing at the shelter door*] Gentleman come to see the shelter, Major. Says he's your father.

BARBARA. All right. Coming. [*Snobby goes back into the shelter, followed by Barbara*].

RUMMY [*stealing across to Bill and addressing him in a subdued voice, but with intense conviction*] I'd av the lor of you, you flat eared pignosed potwalloper, if she'd let me. Youre no gentleman, to hit a lady in the face. [*Bill, with greater things moving in him, takes no notice*].

SHIRLEY [*following her*] Here ! in with you and dont get yourself into more trouble by talking.

RUMMY [*with hauteur*] I aint ad the pleasure o being hintroduced to you, as I can remember. [*She goes into the shelter with the plates*].

SHIRLEY. Thats the—

BILL [*savagely*] Downt you talk to me, d'ye eah ? You lea me alown, or Aw'll do you a mischief. Aw'm not dirt under y o u r feet, ennywy.

SHIRLEY [*calmly*] Dont you be afeerd. You aint such prime company that you need expect to be sought after. [*He is about to go into the shelter when Barbara comes out, with Undershaft on her right*].

BARBARA. Oh, there you are, Mr Shirley ! [*Between them*] This is my father : I told you he was a Secularist, didnt I ? Perhaps youll be able to comfort one another.

UNDERSHAFT [*startled*] A Secularist ! Not the least in the world : on the contrary, a confirmed mystic.

BARBARA. Sorry, I'm sure. By the way, papa, what is your religion ? in case I have to introduce you again.

UNDERSHAFT. My religion ? Well, my dear, I am a Millionaire. That is my religion.

BARBARA. Then I'm afraid you and Mr Shirley wont be able to comfort one another after all. Youre not a Millionaire, are you, Peter ?

SHIRLEY. No ; and proud of it.

UNDERSHAFT [*gravely*] Poverty, my friend, is not a thing to be proud of.

SHIRLEY [*angrily*] Who made your millions for you? Me and my like. Whats kep us poor? Keepin you rich. I wouldnt have your conscience, not for all your income.

UNDERSHAFT. I wouldnt have your income, not for all your conscience, Mr Shirley. [*He goes to the penthouse and sits down on a form*].

BARBARA [*stopping Shirley adroitly as he is about to retort*] You wouldnt think he was my father, would you, Peter? Will you go into the shelter and lend the lasses a hand for a while: we're worked off our feet.

SHIRLEY [*bitterly*] Yes: I'm in their debt for a meal, aint I?

BARBARA. Oh, not because youre in their debt, but for love of them, Peter, for love of them. [*He cannot understand, and is rather scandalized*] There! dont stare at me. In with you; and give that conscience of yours a holiday [*bustling him into the shelter*].

SHIRLEY [*as he goes in*] Ah! it's a pity you never was trained to use your reason, miss. Youd have been a very taking lecturer on Secularism.

Barbara turns to her father.

UNDERSHAFT. Never mind me, my dear. Go about your work; and let me watch it for a while.

BARBARA. All right.

UNDERSHAFT. For instance, whats the matter with that out-patient over there?

BARBARA [*looking at Bill, whose attitude has never changed, and whose expression of brooding wrath has deepened*] Oh, we shall cure him in no time. Just watch. [*She goes over to Bill and waits. He glances up at her and casts his eyes down again, uneasy, but grimmer than ever*]. It would be nice to just stamp on Mog Habbijam's face, wouldnt it, Bill?

BILL [*starting up from the trough in consternation*] It's a loy: Aw never said so. [*She shakes her head*]. Oo taold you wot was in moy mawnd?

BARBARA. Only your new friend.

BILL. Wot new friend ?

BARBARA. The devil, Bill. When he gets round people they get miserable, just like you.

BILL [*with a heartbreaking attempt at devil-may-care cheerfulness*] Aw aint miserable. [*He sits down again, and stretches his legs in an attempt to seem indifferent*].

BARBARA. Well, if youre happy, why dont you look happy, as we do ?

BILL [*his legs curling back in spite of him*] Aw'm eppy enaff, Aw tell you. Woy cawnt you lea me alown ? Wot ev I dan to you ? Aw aint smashed your fice, ev Aw ?

BARBARA [*softly : wooing his soul*] It's not me thats getting at you, Bill.

BILL. Oo else is it ?

BARBARA. Somebody that doesnt intend you to smash women's faces, I suppose. Somebody or something that wants to make a man of you.

BILL [*blustering*] Mike a menn o me ! Aint Aw a menn ? eh ? Oo sez Aw'm not a menn ?

BARBARA. Theres a man in you somewhere, I suppose. But why did he let you hit poor little Jenny Hill ? That wasnt very manly of him, was it ?

BILL [*tormented*] Ev dan wiv it, Aw tell you. Chack it. Aw'm sick o your Jenny Ill and er silly little fice.

BARBARA. Then why do you keep thinking about it ? Why does it keep coming up against you in your mind ? Youre not getting converted, are you ?

BILL [*with conviction*] Not ME. Not lawkly.

BARBARA. Thats right, Bill. Hold out against it. Put out your strength. Dont lets get you cheap. Todger Fairmile said he wrestled for three nights against his salvation harder than he ever wrestled with the Jap at the music hall. He gave in to the Jap when his arm was going to break. But he didnt give in to his salvation until his heart was going to break. Perhaps youll escape that. You havnt any heart, have you ?

BILL. Wot d'ye mean ? Woy aint Aw got a awt the sime as ennybody else ?

BARBARA. A man with a heart wouldnt have bashed poor

little Jenny's face, would he?

BILL [*almost crying*] Ow, will you lea me alown? Ev Aw ever offered to meddle with you, that you cam neggin and provowkin me lawk this? [*He writhes convulsively from his eyes to his toes*].

BARBARA [*with a steady soothing hand on his arm and a gentle voice that never lets him go*] It's your soul thats hurting you, Bill, and not me. Weve been through it all ourselves. Come with us, Bill. [*He looks wildly round*]. To brave manhood on earth and eternal glory in heaven. [*He is on the point of breaking down*]. Come. [*A drum is heard in the shelter; and Bill, with a gasp, escapes from the spell as Barbara turns quickly. Adolphus enters from the shelter with a big drum*]. Oh! there you are, Dolly. Let me introduce a new friend of mine, Mr Bill Walker. This is my bloke, Bill: Mr Cusins. [*Cusins salutes with his drumstick*].

BILL. Gowin to merry im?

BARBARA. Yes.

BILL [*fervently*] Gawd elp im! Gaw-aw-aw-awd elp im!

BARBARA. Why? Do you think he wont be happy with me?

BILL. Awve aony ed to stend it for a mawnin: e'll ev to stend it for a lawftawm.

CUSINS. That is a frightful reflection, Mr Walker. But I cant tear myself away from her.

BILL. Well, Aw ken. [*To Barbara*] Eah! do you knaow where Aw'm gowin to, and wot Aw'm gowin to do?

BARBARA. Yes: youre going to heaven; and youre coming back here before the week's out to tell me so.

BILL. You loy. Aw'm gowin to Keninntahn, to spit in Todger Fairmawl's eye. Aw beshed Jenny Ill's fice; an nar Aw'll git me aown fice beshed and cam beck and shaow it to er. Ee'll itt me ardern Aw itt er. Thatll mike us square. [*To Adolphus*] Is thet fair or is it not? Youre a genlmn: you oughter knaow.

BARBARA. Two black eyes wont make one white one, Bill.

BILL. Aw didnt awst you. Cawnt you never keep your mahth shut? Oy awst the genlmn.

CUSINS [*reflectively*] Yes : I think youre right, Mr Walker. Yes : I should do it. It's curious : it's exactly what an ancient Greek would have done.

BARBARA. But what good will it do ?

CUSINS. Well, it will give Mr Fairmile some exercise ; and it will satisfy Mr Walker's soul.

BILL. Rot ! there aint nao sach a thing as a saoul. Ah kin you tell wevver Awve a saoul or not ? You never seen it.

BARBARA. Ive seen it hurting you when you went against it.

BILL [*with compressed aggravation*] If you was maw gel and took the word aht o me mahth lawk thet, Aw'd give you sathink youd feel urtin, Aw would. [*To Adolphus*] You tike maw tip, mite. Stop er jawr ; or youll doy afoah your tawm. [*With intense expression*] Wore aht : thets wot youll be : wore aht. [*He goes away through the gate*].

CUSINS [*looking after him*] I wonder !

BARBARA. Dolly ! [*indignant, in her mother's manner*].

CUSINS. Yes, my dear, it's very wearing to be in love with you. If it lasts, I quite think I shall die young.

BARBARA. Should you mind ?

CUSINS. Not at all. [*He is suddenly softened, and kisses her over the drum, evidently not for the first time, as people cannot kiss over a big drum without practice. Undershaft coughs*].

BARBARA. It's all right, papa, weve not forgotten you. Dolly : explain the place to papa : I havnt time. [*She goes busily into the shelter*].

Undershaft and Adolphus now have the yard to themselves. Undershaft, seated on a form, and still keenly attentive, looks hard at Adolphus. Adolphus looks hard at him.

UNDERSHAFT. I fancy you guess something of what is in my mind, Mr Cusins. [*Cusins flourishes his drumsticks as if in the act of beating a lively rataplan, but makes no sound*]. Exactly so. But suppose Barbara finds you out !

CUSINS. You know, I do not admit that I am imposing on

Barbara. I am quite genuinely interested in the views of the Salvation Army. The fact is, I am a sort of collector of religions; and the curious thing is that I find I can believe them all. By the way, have you any religion?

UNDERSHAFT. Yes.

CUSINS. Anything out of the common?

UNDERSHAFT. Only that there are two things necessary to Salvation.

CUSINS [*disappointed, but polite*] Ah, the Church Catechism. Charles Lomax also belongs to the Established Church.

UNDERSHAFT. The two things are—

CUSINS. Baptism and—

UNDERSHAFT. No. Money and gunpowder.

CUSINS [*surprised, but interested*] That is the general opinion of our governing classes. The novelty is in hearing any man confess it.

UNDERSHAFT. Just so.

CUSINS. Excuse me: is there any place in your religion for honor, justice, truth, love, mercy and so forth?

UNDERSHAFT. Yes: they are the graces and luxuries of a rich, strong, and safe life.

CUSINS. Suppose one is forced to choose between them and money or gunpowder?

UNDERSHAFT. Choose money and gunpowder; for without enough of both you cannot afford the others.

CUSINS. That is your religion?

UNDERSHAFT. Yes.

The cadence of this reply makes a full close in the conversation. Cusins twists his face dubiously and contemplates Undershaft. Undershaft contemplates him.

CUSINS. Barbara wont stand that. You will have to choose between your religion and Barbara.

UNDERSHAFT. So will you, my friend. She will find out that that drum of yours is hollow.

CUSINS. Father Undershaft: you are mistaken: I am a sincere Salvationist. You do not understand the Salvation Army. It is the army of joy, of love, of courage: it has banished the fear and remorse and despair of the old hell-ridden evangelical sects: it marches to fight the devil with trumpet and drum, with music and dancing, with banner and palm, as becomes a sally from heaven by its happy garrison. It picks the waster out of the public house and makes a man of him: it finds a worm wriggling in a back kitchen, and lo! a woman! Men and women of rank too, sons and daughters of the Highest. It takes the poor professor of Greek, the most artificial and self-suppressed of human creatures, from his meal of roots, and lets loose the rhapsodist in him; reveals the true worship of Dionysos to him; sends him down the public street drumming dithyrambs [*he plays a thundering flourish on the drum*].

UNDERSHAFT. You will alarm the shelter.

CUSINS. Oh, they are accustomed to these sudden ecstasies. However, if the drum worries you—[*he pockets the drum-sticks; unhooks the drum; and stands it on the ground opposite the gateway*].

UNDERSHAFT. Thank you. And now to business.

CUSINS. Pardon me. We are discussing religion. Why go back to such an uninteresting and unimportant subject as business?

UNDERSHAFT. Religion is our business at present, because it is through religion alone that we can win Barbara.

CUSINS. Have you, too, fallen in love with Barbara?

UNDERSHAFT. Yes, with a father's love.

CUSINS. A father's love for a grown-up daughter is the most dangerous of all infatuations. I apologize for mentioning my own pale, coy, mistrustful fancy in the same breath with it.

UNDERSHAFT. Keep to the point. We have to win her; and we are neither of us Methodists.

CUSINS. That doesnt matter. The power Barbara wields here—the power that wields Barbara herself—is not Calvinism, not Presbyterianism, not Methodism—

UNDERSHAFT. Not Greek Paganism either, eh?

CUSINS. I admit that. Barbara is quite original in her religion.

UNDERSHAFT [*triumphantly*] Aha! Barbara Undershaft would be. Her inspiration comes from within herself.

CUSINS. How do you suppose it got there?

UNDERSHAFT [*in towering excitement*] It is the Undershaft inheritance. I shall hand on my torch to my daughter. She shall make my converts and preach my gospel—

CUSINS. What! Money and gunpowder!

UNDERSHAFT. Yes, money and gunpowder. Freedom and power. Command of life and command of death.

CUSINS [*urbanely: trying to bring him down to earth*] This is extremely interesting, Mr Undershaft. Of course you know that you are mad.

UNDERSHAFT [*with redoubled force*] And you?

CUSINS. Oh, mad as a hatter. You are welcome to my secret since I have discovered yours. But I am astonished. Can a madman make cannons?

UNDERSHAFT. Would anyone else than a madman make them? And now [*with surging energy*] question for question. Can a sane man translate Euripides?

CUSINS. No.

UNDERSHAFT [*seizing him by the shoulder*] Can a sane woman make a man of a waster or a woman of a worm?

CUSINS [*reeling before the storm*] Father Colossus—Mammoth Millionaire—

UNDERSHAFT [*pressing him*] Are there two mad people or three in this Salvation shelter today?

CUSINS. You mean Barbara is as mad as we are?

UNDERSHAFT [*pushing him lightly off and resuming his equanimity suddenly and completely*] Pooh, Professor! let us call things by their proper names. I am a millionaire; you are a poet; Barbara is a savior of souls. What have we three to do with the common mob of slaves and idolaters? [*He sits down again with a shrug of contempt for the mob*].

CUSINS. Take care! Barbara is in love with the common people. So am I. Have you never felt the romance of that love?

UNDERSHAFT [*cold and sardonic*] Have you ever been in love with Poverty, like St Francis? Have you ever been in love with Dirt, like St Simeon ? Have you ever been in love with disease and suffering, like our nurses and philanthropists ? Such passions are not virtues, but the most unnatural of all the vices. This love of the common people may please an earl's granddaughter and a university professor ; but I have been a common man and a poor man ; and it has no romance for me. Leave it to the poor to pretend that poverty is a blessing : leave it to the coward to make a religion of his cowardice by preaching humility : we know better than that. We three must stand together above the common people : how else can we help their children to climb up beside us ? Barbara must belong to us, not to the Salvation Army.

CUSINS. Well, I can only say that if you think you will get her away from the Salvation Army by talking to her as you have been talking to me, you dont know Barbara.

UNDERSHAFT. My friend : I never ask for what I can buy.

CUSINS [*in a white fury*] Do I understand you to imply that you can buy Barbara ?

UNDERSHAFT. No ; but I can buy the Salvation Army.

CUSINS. Quite impossible.

UNDERSHAFT. You shall see. All religious organizations exist by selling themselves to the rich.

CUSINS. Not the Army. That is the Church of the poor.

UNDERSHAFT. All the more reason for buying it.

CUSINS. I dont think you quite know what the Army does for the poor.

UNDERSHAFT. Oh yes I do. It draws their teeth : that is enough for me as a man of business.

CUSINS. Nonsense ! It makes them sober—

UNDERSHAFT. I prefer sober workmen. The profits are larger.

CUSINS—honest—

UNDERSHAFT. Honest workmen are the most economical.

CUSINS—attached to their homes—

UNDERSHAFT. So much the better : they will put up with anything sooner than change their shop.

CUSINS—happy—

UNDERSHAFT. An invaluable safeguard against revolution.

CUSINS—unselfish—

UNDERSHAFT. Indifferent to their own interests, which suits me exactly.

CUSINS—with their thoughts on heavenly things—

UNDERSHAFT [*rising*] And not on Trade Unionism nor Socialism. Excellent.

CUSINS [*revolted*] You really are an infernal old rascal.

UNDERSHAFT [*indicating Peter Shirley, who has just come from the shelter and strolled dejectedly down the yard between them*] And this is an honest man !

SHIRLEY. Yes ; and wot ev I got by it ? [*he passes on bitterly and sits on the form, in the corner of the penthouse*].

Snobby Price, beaming sanctimoniously, and Jenny Hill, with a tambourine full of coppers, come from the shelter and go to the drum, on which Jenny begins to count the money.

UNDERSHAFT [*replying to Shirley*] Oh, your employers must have got a good deal by it from first to last. [*He sits on the table, with one foot on the side form, Cusins, overwhelmed, sits down on the same form nearer the shelter. Barbara comes from the shelter to the middle of the yard. She is excited and a little overwrought*].

BARBARA. Weve just had a splendid experience meeting at the other gate in Cripps's lane. Ive hardly ever seen them so much moved as they were by your confession, Mr Price.

PRICE. I could almost be glad of my past wickedness if I could believe that it would elp to keep hathers stright.

BARBARA. So it will, Snobby. How much, Jenny ?

JENNY. Four and tenpence, Major.

BARBARA. Oh Snobby, if you had given your poor mother just one more kick, we should have got the whole five shillings !

PRICE. If she heard you say that, miss, she'd be sorry I didnt. But I'm glad. Oh what a joy it will be to her when she hears I'm saved !

UNDERSHAFT. Shall I contribute the odd twopence, Barbara ? The millionaire's mite, eh ? [*He takes a couple of pennies from his pocket*].

BARBARA. How did you make that twopence?

UNDERSHAFT. As usual. By selling cannons, torpedoes, submarines, and my new patent Grand Duke hand grenade.

BARBARA. Put it back in your pocket. You cant buy your salvation here for twopence: you must work it out.

UNDERSHAFT. Is twopence not enough? I can afford a little more, if you press me.

BARBARA. Two million millions would not be enough. There is bad blood on your hands; and nothing but good blood can cleanse them. Money is no use. Take it away. [*She turns to Cusins*]. Dolly: you must write another letter for me to the papers. [*He makes a wry face*]. Yes: I know you dont like it; but it must be done. The starvation this winter is beating us: everybody is unemployed. The General says we must close this shelter if we cant get more money. I force the collections at the meetings until I am ashamed: dont I, Snobby?

PRICE. It's a fair treat to see you work it, miss. The way you got them up from three-and-six to four-and-ten with that hymn, penny by penny and verse by verse, was a caution. Not a Cheap Jack on Mile End Waste could touch you at it.

BARBARA. Yes; but I wish we could do without it. I am getting at last to think more of the collection than of the people's souls. And what are those hatfuls of pence and halfpence? We want thousands! tens of thousands! hundreds of thousands! I want to convert people, not to be always begging for the Army in a way I'd die sooner than beg for myself.

UNDERSHAFT [*in profound irony*] Genuine unselfishness is capable of anything, my dear.

BARBARA [*unsuspectingly, as she turns away to take the money from the drum and put it in a cash bag she carries*] Yes, isnt it? [*Undershaft looks sardonically at Cusins*].

CUSINS [*aside to Undershaft*] Mephistopheles! Machiavelli!

BARBARA [*tears coming into her eyes as she ties the bag and pockets it*] How are we to feed them? I cant talk religion to a man with bodily hunger in his eyes. [*Almost breaking down*] It's frightful.

JENNY [*running to her*] Major, dear—

BARBARA [*rebounding*] No: dont comfort me. It will be all right. We shall get the money.

UNDERSHAFT. How?

JENNY. By praying for it, of course. Mrs Baines says she prayed for it last night; and she has never prayed for it in vain: never once. [*She goes to the gate and looks out into the street*].

BARBARA [*who has dried her eyes and regained her composure*] By the way, dad, Mrs Baines has come to march with us to our big meeting this afternoon; and she is very anxious to meet you, for some reason or other. Perhaps she'll convert you.

UNDERSHAFT. I shall be delighted, my dear.

JENNY [*at the gate: excitedly*] Major! Major! heres that man back again.

BARBARA. What man?

JENNY. The man that hit me. Oh, I hope hes coming back to join us.

Bill comes through the gate, his hands deep in his pockets and his chin sunk between his shoulders, like a cleaned-out gambler. He halts between Barbara and the drum.

BARBARA. Hullo, Bill! Back already!

BILL [*nagging at her*] Bin talkin ever sence, ev you?

BARBARA. Pretty nearly. Well, has Todger paid you out for poor Jenny's jaw?

BILL. No he aint.

BARBARA. I thought your jacket looked a bit snowy.

BILL. So it is snaowy. You want to know where the snaow come from, dont you?

BARBARA. Yes.

BILL. Well, Awll teoll you. [*Bill, being a cockney proletarian, pronounces l as ee-aw, and is himself called Beeyaw by his intimates*].

And what he tells her is this. In a street in Canning Town, an eastern suburb of London where the main thoroughfare is broad and spacious but the people poor and the shops cheap, Todger Fairmile and Mog Habbijam are holding a Salvation Army meeting at a corner near a flourishing public house. As it is Sunday morning the public house is closed ; and Todger and Mog, being recent converts, have not yet found out that when its doors open it will profit by a crowd, no matter how that crowd has been induced to assemble. It is an attractive meeting. The brass band, ten strong, plays very handsomely ; and its leader, who plays the soprano cornet (the old cornetto revived by the Army, and the most difficult instrument in the band) is quite a virtuoso. Mog, a shapely lass with a natural border of red gold hair under her bonnet, is well worth looking at ; and Todger, the ex-wrestler, in the prime of his athletic youth, is not a figure to be passed by without stopping on an idle Sunday morning. The crowd is therefore not at all an exclusively pious one : all sorts of people are looking and listening, except ladies and gentlemen, who are not indigenous in Canning Town—or Kennintahn, as the natives call it. Mog, radiant in the first flush of her conversion, is addressing it.

MOG. Dear friends : we shall have another hymn presently. You dont know how it warms our hearts to hear so many of you joining in and knowing the dear words. I want to share my happiness with you. It is within your reach : you have only to stretch out your hands and take it. Listen to me, dear friends. A month ago I was the unhappiest girl in London. I wanted pleasure, pleasure, pleasure. I drank : I swore : I was unclean in my mind and in my body. And I was so miserable that I would walk out with any man, if he had money enough to treat me in every public house we passed. Not one of you would have let your daughters speak to me or your sons be seen with me. I thought I was a grand girl enjoying myself all the time. And I was lost and miserable, miserable, miserable. One day when I went to a public house for another drink, I found an Army meeting going on outside.

Just as you have here. I stopped to laugh and mock at it. Just as some of you are stopping here today. Do you know who was conducting that meeting? Here he is: Sergeant Todger Fairmile: the greatest fighter in the Isle of Dogs. I laughed and mocked and put out my tongue at him; but he saw how unhappy I was. "You poor dirty unhappy little slut" he said "God has chosen you this day to have your sins cleansed and your soul lifted out of the mire of hell and saved." And he put his hand on me; and it was as strong as the hand of God, not because his hand is so strong, but because it was really the hand of God. And from that hour heaven opened to me and I became as happy as an angel. Oh, dear friends, dont you envy me? If that could happen to such a wretch as I was, how much more easily will it happen to you! Dear Sergeant: tell them. My heart's overflowing: I cant speak.

TODGER. You all know who I am, Todger Fairmile, champion wrestler, boxer, and swimmer. Some of you have put money on me and won it.

BYSTANDER. Yes; and some of us put our money the other way and lost it.

TODGER. Youll lose no more that way: I shall ask you for a penny or two in the lass's tambourine presently. Ive been promoted sergeant in the Salvation Army.

ANOTHER BYSTANDER. Yes: its easier than fighting, isnt it?

TODGER. No, my friend, it's not easier; but it's ever so much happier. And who told you that I have given up fighting? I was born a fighter; and, please God, I'll die a fighter. But the ring was too small for a champion like me. It was no satisfaction to me to knock out some poor fellow, or to get his shoulders down on the mat for a purse of money. It was too easy; and there was no future in it for either of us, though we were both facing eternity. One day I gave an exhibition spar for the benefit of a charity. Our General was there; and I was introduced to her. She said I was a wonderful young man; and she asked me was I saved.

"No" says I "but I can go fifteen rounds with Tommy Farr if youll put up the money." "Of course you can," she says. "God built you big enough for a trifle like that. But will you go, not fifteen rounds, but eternity, with the devil for no money at all? He is the champion the Army has to fight. Have you pluck enough for that?" I tried hard to make light of it; but it stuck; and a week after I took the count for the first time and joined up. And now I fight the devil all the time; and I'll say for him that he fights fairer and harder than some champions I have tackled. But God is against him. And in that sign we shall conquer. And now shall we have another hymn?

He turns to the band who take up their instruments. The Salvationists open their hymnbooks.

While Todger's back is turned Bill Walker pushes his way through the crowd and takes Todger by the arm.

BILL. Youre Todger Firemawl, are you?

TODGER. Sergeant Fairmile, at your service, sir.

BILL. You took awy maw judy, did you? Nime of Mog Ebbijam.

MOG. Bill!! Dont you know me?

BILL. Blaow me! Its er voice. Wot ev you dan t'yseeawf? Wotz e dan to you?

MOG. Sergeant: it's Bill Walker, that was my bloke. And I'm so changed he doesnt know me.

TODGER. We'll make the same change in you, Bill. Is that what youve come for?

BILL [*turning to Todger*] Awv cam to ev me fice chynged rawt enaff; an' youre the menn that's gaoin to chynge it. Tike thet. [*He spits in Todger's face*]. Nah, eah's maw jawr. Itt it. Itt it your best. Brike it.

TODGER. Oh, that I should be found worthy to be spit upon for the Gospel's sake!

MOG. You shouldnt have done that, Bill. Youve spit in the face of your salvation.

BILL [*to Todger*] Listen eah you. D'yew knaow a slip of a girl nimed Jinny Ill?

TODGER. We do. Has she converted you?

BILL. Keep your mawnd orf this conversion business and listen to wot Awm teollin you. Aw browk Jinny Ill's jawr this mawnin.

TODGER. No you didnt, Bill. It's not so easy to break a jaw as you think. You havnt the punch for it. You hit her in the face like the fine bold fellow you are; and now you want to forgive yourself; and you find you cant unless I give you your blow back harder than you can hit. [*To the crowd*] Dear friends: this man is on the way to his salvation. Let us kneel down and pray for him. [*The Salvationists kneel. Bill and Todger remain standing*]. Kneel down, Bill.

BILL. [*furiously*] The hell I will!

Todger throws him down on his face; and kneels on his shoulders. Mog kneels beside him. Both pray devoutly with bent heads while the band plays a hymn.

BILL. Eah! wot you think Awm mide of?

MOG [*praying*] Oh Lord: break his stubborn spirit; but dont urt iz dear eart.

BILL [*scrambling up and feeling his ribs*] Never you mawnd maw deah awt. Wot abaht maw ribs? you and your fourteen staown blowk! [*Roar of laughter from the profane section of the crowd*] Larf awy: Aw see Aw kin git naow jastice eah. Well, Aw'll settle wiv Jinny Ill in me aown wy, spawt o the lot o you. [*He elbows his way through the crowd, and trudges off on his way back to the West Ham shelter*].

And so ends Bill's account to Barbara of what happened to him in Canning Town as he told it to her and to the rest in the yard of the West Ham shelter.

BILL [*finishing his tale*] Sao naow you knaow all the good that move dan me.

BARBARA [*her eyes dancing*] Wish I'd been there, Bill.

BILL. Yus: youd a got in a hextra bit o talk on me, wouldnt you?

JENNY. I'm so sorry, Mr Walker.

BILL [*fiercely*] Downt you gaow bein sorry for me: youve no call. Listen eah. Aw browk your jawr.

JENNY. No, it didnt hurt me: indeed it didnt, except for a

moment. It was only that I was frightened.

BILL. Aw downt want to be forgive be you, or be ennybody. Wot Aw did Aw'll py for. Aw trawd to gat me aown jawr browk to settisfaw you—

JENNY [*distressed*] Oh no—

BILL [*impatiently*] Teoll y' Aw did : cawnt you listen to wots bein taold you ? All Aw got be it was bein mide a sawt of in the pablic street for me pines. Weoll, if Aw cawnt settisfaw you one wy, Aw ken anather. Listen eah ! Aw ed two quid sived agen the frost ; an Awve a pahnd of it left. A mite o mawn last week ed words with the judy e's gaowin to merry. E give er wot-for ; an e's bin fawnd fifteen bob. E ed a rawt to itt er cause they was gaowin to be merrid ; but Aw ednt nao rawt to itt you ; sao put anather fawv bob on an call it a pahnd's worth. [*He produces a sovereign*]. Eahs the manney. Tike it ; and lets ev no more o your forgivin an pryin and your Mijor jawrin me. Let wot Aw dan be dan an pide for ; and let there be a end of it.

JENNY. Oh, I couldnt take it, Mr Walker. But if you would give a shilling or two to poor Rummy Mitchens ! you really did hurt her ; and she's old.

BILL [*contemptuously*] Not lawkly. Aw'd give her anather as soon as look at er. Let her ev the lawr o me as she threatened ! She aint forgiven me : not mach. Wot Aw dan to er is not on me mawnd—wot she [*indicating Barbara*] mawt call on me conscience—no more than stickin a pig. It's this Christian gime o yours that Aw wownt ev plyed agen me : this bloomin forgivin an neggin an jawrin that mikes a menn thet sore that iz lawf's a burdn to im. Aw waownt ev it, Aw teoll you ; sao tike your manney and stop thraowin your silly barshed fice hap agen me.

JENNY. Major : may I take a little of it for the Army ?

BARBARA. No : the Army is not to be bought. We want your soul, Bill ; and we'll take nothing less.

BILL [*bitterly*] Aw knaow. Me an maw few shillins is not good enaff for you. Youre a earl's grendorter, you are. Nathink less than a anderd pahnd for you.

UNDERSHAFT. Come, Barbara! you could do a great deal of good with a hundred pounds. If you will set this gentleman's mind at ease by taking his pound, I will give the other ninety-nine.

Bill, dazed by such opulence, instinctively touches his cap.

BARBARA. Oh, youre too extravagant, papa. Bill offers twenty pieces of silver. All you need offer is the other ten. That will make the standard price to buy anybody who's for sale. I'm not; and the Army's not. [*To Bill*] Youll never have another quiet moment, Bill, until you come round to us. You cant stand out against your salvation.

BILL [*sullenly*] Aw cawnt stend aht agen music awl wrastlers and awtful tangued women. Awve offered to py. Aw can do no more. Tike it or leave it. There it is. [*He throws the sovereign on the drum, and sits down on the horse-trough. The coin fascinates Snobby Price, who takes an early opportunity of dropping his cap on it*].

Mrs Baines comes from the shelter. She is dressed as a Salvation Army Commissioner. She is an earnest looking woman of forty, with a caressing, urgent voice, and an appealing manner.

BARBARA. This is my father, Mrs Baines. [*Undershaft comes from the table, taking his hat off with marked civility*]. Try what you can do with him. He wont listen to me, because he remembers what a fool I was when I was a baby. [*She leaves them together and chats with Jenny*].

MRS BAINES. Have you been shewn over the shelter, Mr Undershaft? You know the work we're doing, of course.

UNDERSHAFT [*very civilly*] The whole nation knows it, Mrs Baines.

MRS BAINES. No, sir: the whole nation does not know it, or we should not be crippled as we are for want of money to carry our work through the length and breadth of the land. Let me tell you that there would have been rioting this winter in London but for us.

UNDERSHAFT. You really think so?

MRS BAINES. I know it. I remember 1886, when you rich

gentlemen hardened your hearts against the cry of the poor. They broke the windows of your clubs in Pall Mall.

UNDERSHAFT [*gleaming with approval of their method*] And the Mansion House Fund went up next day from thirty thousand pounds to seventy-nine thousand! I remember quite well.

MRS BAINES. Well, wont you help me to get at the people? They wont break windows then. Come here, Price. Let me shew you to this gentleman [*Price comes to be inspected*]. Do you remember the window breaking?

PRICE. My ole father thought it was the revolution, maam.

MRS BAINES. Would you break windows now?

PRICE. Oh no, maam. The windows of eaven av bin opened to me. I know now that the rich man is a sinner like myself.

RUMMY [*appearing above at the loft door*] Snobby Price!

SNOBBY. Wot is it?

RUMMY. Your mother's askin for you at the other gate in Cripps's Lane. She's heard about your confession [*Price turns pale*].

MRS BAINES. Go, Mr Price, and pray with her.

JENNY. You can go through the shelter, Snobby.

PRICE [*to Mrs Baines*] I couldnt face her now, maam, with all the weight of my sins fresh on me. Tell her she'll find her son at ome, waitin for her in prayer. [*He skulks off through the gate, incidentally stealing the sovereign on his way out by picking up his cap from the drum*].

MRS BAINES [*with swimming eyes*] You see how we take the anger and the bitterness against you out of their hearts, Mr Undershaft.

UNDERSHAFT. It is certainly most convenient and gratifying to all large employers of labor, Mrs Baines.

MRS BAINES. Barbara: Jenny: I have good news: most wonderful news. [*Jenny runs to her*]. My prayers have been answered. I told you they would, Jenny, didnt I?

JENNY. Yes, yes.

BARBARA [*moving nearer to the drum*] Have we got money

enough to keep the shelter open?

MRS BAINES. I hope we shall have enough to keep all the shelters open. Lord Saxmundham has promised us five thousand pounds—

BARBARA. Hooray!

JENNY. Glory!

MRS BAINES. —if—

BARBARA. "If!" If what?

MRS BAINES —if five other gentlemen will give a thousand each to make it up to ten thousand.

BARBARA. Who is Lord Saxmundham? I never heard of him.

UNDERSHAFT [*who has pricked up his ears at the peer's name, and is now watching Barbara curiously*] A new creation, my dear. You have heard of Sir Horace Bodger?

BARBARA. Bodger! Do you mean the distiller? Bodger's whisky!

UNDERSHAFT. That is the man. He is one of the greatest of our public benefactors. He restored the cathedral at Hakington. They made him a baronet for that. He gave half a million to the funds of his party: they made him a baron for that.

SHIRLEY. What will they give him for the five thousand?

UNDERSHAFT. There is nothing left to give him. So the five thousand, I should think, is to save his soul.

MRS BAINES. Heaven grant it may! Oh Mr Undershaft, you have some very rich friends. Cant you help us towards the other five thousand? We are going to hold a great meeting this afternoon at the Assembly Hall in the Mile End Road. If I could only announce that one gentleman had come forward to support Lord Saxmundham, others would follow. Dont you know somebody? couldnt you? wouldnt you? [*her eyes fill with tears*] oh, think of those poor people, Mr Undershaft: think of how much it means to them, and how little to a great man like you.

UNDERSHAFT [*sardonically gallant*] Mrs Baines: you are irresistible. I cant disappoint you; and I cant deny myself the satisfaction of making Bodger pay up. You shall have your five thousand pounds.

MRS BAINES. Thank God !

UNDERSHAFT. You dont thank me ?

MRS BAINES. Oh sir, dont try to be cynical : dont be ashamed of being a good man. The Lord will bless you abundantly ; and our prayers will be like a strong fortification round you all the days of your life. [*With a touch of caution*] You will let me have the cheque to shew at the meeting, wont you ? Jenny : go in and fetch a pen and ink. [*Jenny runs to the shelter door*].

UNDERSHAFT. Do not disturb Miss Hill : I have a fountain pen. [*Jenny halts. He sits on the table and writes the cheque. Cusins rises to make room for him. They all watch him silently*].

BILL [*cynically, aside to Barbara, his voice and accent horribly debased*] Wot prawce selvytion nah ?

BARBARA. Stop. [*Undershaft stops writing : they all turn to her in surprise*]. Mrs Baines : are you really going to take this money ?

MRS BAINES [*astonished*] Why not, dear ?

BARBARA. Why not ! Do you know what my father is ? Have you forgotten that Lord Saxmundham is Bodger the whisky man ? Do you remember how we implored the County Council to stop him from writing Bodger's Whisky in letters of fire against the sky ; so that the poor drink-ruined creatures on the Embankment could not wake up from their snatches of sleep without being reminded of their deadly thirst by that wicked sky sign ? Do you know that the worst thing I have had to fight here is not the devil, but Bodger, Bodger, Bodger, with his whisky, his distilleries, and his tied houses ? Are you going to make our shelter another tied house for him, and ask me to keep it ?

BILL. Rotten dranken whisky it is too.

MRS BAINES. Dear Barbara : Lord Saxmundham has a soul to be saved like any of us. If heaven has found the way to make a good use of his money, are we to set ourselves up against the answer to our prayers ?

BARBARA. I know he has a soul to be saved. Let him come down here; and I'll do my best to help him to his salvation. But he wants to send his cheque down to buy us, and go on being as wicked as ever.

UNDERSHAFT [*with a reasonableness which Cusins alone perceives to be ironical*] My dear Barbara: alcohol is a very necessary article. It heals the sick—

BARBARA. It does nothing of the sort.

UNDERSHAFT. Well, it assists the doctor: that is perhaps a less questionable way of putting it. It makes life bearable to millions of people who could not endure their existence if they were quite sober. It enables Parliament to do things at eleven at night that no sane person would do at eleven in the morning. Is it Bodger's fault that this inestimable gift is deplorably abused by less than one per cent of the poor? [*He turns again to the table; signs the cheque; and crosses it*].

MRS BAINES. Barbara: will there be less drinking or more if all those poor souls we are saving come tomorrow and find the doors of our shelters shut in their faces? Lord Saxmundham gives us the money to stop drinking —to take his own business from him.

CUSINS [*impishly*] Pure self-sacrifice on Bodger's part, clearly! Bless dear Bodger! [*Barbara almost breaks down as Adolphus, too, fails her*].

UNDERSHAFT [*tearing out the cheque and pocketing the book as he rises and goes past Cusins to Mrs Baines*] I also, Mrs Baines, may claim a little disinterestedness. Think of my business! think of the widows and orphans! the men and lads torn to pieces with shrapnel and poisoned with lyddite! [*Mrs Baines shrinks; but he goes on remorselessly*] the oceans of blood, not one drop of which is shed in a really just cause! the ravaged crops! the peaceful peasants forced, women and men, to till their fields under the fire of opposing armies on pain of starvation! the bad blood of the fierce little cowards at home who egg on others to fight for the gratification of their national vanity! All this makes money for me: I am never richer, never busier than when the papers are full of it. Well, it is your work to preach peace on earth and goodwill to men. [*Mrs Baines's face lights up again*]. Every convert you make is a vote against war. [*Her lips move in prayer*]. Yet I give you this money to help you to hasten my own commercial ruin. [*He gives her the cheque*].

CUSINS [*mounting the form in an ecstasy of mischief*] The millennium will be inaugurated by the unselfishness of Undershaft and Bodger. Oh be joyful ! [*He takes the drum-sticks from his pocket and flourishes them*].

MRS BAINES [*taking the cheque*] The longer I live the more proof I see that there is an Infinite Goodness that turns everything to the work of salvation sooner or later. Who would have thought that any good could have come out of war and drink ? And yet their profits are brought today to the feet of salvation to do its blessed work. [*She is affected to tears*].

JENNY [*running to Mrs Baines and throwing her arms round her*] Oh dear ! how blessed, how glorious it all is !

CUSINS [*in a convulsion of irony*] Let us seize this unspeakable moment. Let us march to the great meeting at once. Excuse me just an instant. [*He rushes into the shelter. Jenny takes her tambourine from the drum head*].

MRS BAINES. Mr Undershaft : have you ever seen a thousand people fall on their knees with one impulse and pray ? Come with us to the meeting. Barbara shall tell them that the Army is saved, and saved through you.

CUSINS [*returning impetuously from the shelter with a flag and a trombone, and coming between Mrs Baines and Undershaft*] You shall carry the flag down the first street, Mrs Baines [*he gives her the flag*]. Mr Undershaft is a gifted trombonist : he shall intone an Olympian diapason to the West Ham Salvation March. [*Aside to Undershaft, as he forces the trombone on him*] Blow, Machiavelli, blow.

UNDERSHAFT [*aside to him, as he takes the trombone*] The trumpet in Zion ! [*Cusins rushes to the drum, which he takes up and puts on. Undershaft continues, aloud*] I will do my best. I could vamp a bass if I knew the tune.

CUSINS. It is a wedding chorus from one of Donizetti's operas; but we have converted it. We convert everything to good here, including Bodger. You remember the chorus. "For thee immense rejoicing—immenso giubilo—immenso giubilo." [*With drum obbligato*] Rum tum ti tum tum, tum tum ti ta—

BARBARA. Dolly: you are breaking my heart.

CUSINS. What is a broken heart more or less here? Dionysos Undershaft has descended. I am possessed.

MRS BAINES. Come, Barbara: I must have my dear Major to carry the flag with me.

JENNY. Yes, yes, Major darling.

CUSINS [*snatches the tambourine out of Jenny's hand and mutely offers it to Barbara*].

BARBARA [*coming forward a little as she puts the offer behind her with a shudder, whilst Cusins recklessly tosses the tambourine back to Jenny, and goes to the gate*] I cant come.

JENNY. Not come!

MRS BAINES [*with tears in her eyes*] Barbara: do you think I am wrong to take the money?

BARBARA [*impulsively going to her and kissing her*] No, no: God help you, dear, you must: you are saving the Army. Go; and may you have a great meeting!

JENNY. But arnt you coming?

BARBARA. No. [*She begins taking off the silver S brooch from her collar*].

MRS BAINES. Barbara: what are you doing?

JENNY. Why are you taking your badge off? You cant be going to leave us, Major.

BARBARA [*quietly*] Father: come here.

UNDERSHAFT [*coming to her*] My dear! [*Seeing that she is going to pin the badge on his collar, he retreats to the penthouse in some alarm*].

BARBARA [*following him*] Dont be frightened. [*She pins the badge on and steps back towards the table, shewing him to the others*] There! It's not much for £5000, is it?

MRS BAINES. Barbara: if you wont come and pray with us,

promise me you will pray for us.

BARBARA. I cant pray now. Perhaps I shall never pray again.

MRS BAINES. Barbara!

JENNY. Major!

BARBARA [*almost delirious*] I cant bear any more. Quick march!

CUSINS [*calling to the procession in the street outside*] Off we go. Play up, there! Immenso giubilo. [*He gives the time with his drum; and the band strikes up the march, which rapidly becomes more distant as the procession moves briskly away*].

MRS BAINES. I must go, dear. Youre overworked: you will be all right tomorrow. We'll never lose you. Now Jenny: step out with the old flag. Blood and Fire! [*She marches out through the gate with her flag*].

JENNY. Glory Hallelujah! [*flourishing her tambourine and marching*].

UNDERSHAFT [*to Cusins, as he marches out past him easing the slide of his trombone*] "My ducats and my daughter"!

CUSINS [*following him out*] Money and gunpowder!

BARBARA. Drunkenness and Murder! My God: why hast thou forsaken me?

She sinks on the form with her face buried in her hands. The march passes away into silence. Bill Walker steals across to her.

BILL [*taunting*] Wot prawce selvytion nah?

SHIRLEY. Dont you hit her when she's down.

BILL. She itt me wen aw wiz dahn. Waw shouldnt Aw git a bit o me aown beck?

BARBARA [*raising her head*] I didnt take your money, Bill. [*She crosses the yard to the gate and turns her back on the two men to hide her face from them*].

BILL [*sneering after her*] Naow, it warnt enaff for you. [*Turning to the drum, he misses the money*] Ellow! If you aint took it sammun else ez. Weres it gorn? Bly me if Jenny Ill didnt tike it arter all!

RUMMY [*screaming at him from the left*] You lie, you dirty blackguard! Snobby Price pinched it off the drum when he took up his cap. I was up here all the time an see im do it.

BILL. Wot! Stowl maw manney! Waw didnt you call thiof on him, you silly aold macker you?

RUMMY. To serve you aht for ittin me acrost the fice. It's cost y'pahnd, that az. [*Raising a pæan of squalid triumph*] I done you. I'm even with you. Ive ad it aht o y— [*Bill snatches up Shirley's mug and hurls it at her. She slams the loft door and vanishes. The mug smashes against the door and falls in fragments*].

BILL [*beginning to chuckle*] Tell us, aol menn, wot o'clock this mawnin was it wen im as they call Snobby Prawce was sived?

BARBARA [*turning to him more composedly, and with unspoiled sweetness*] About half past twelve, Bill. And he pinched your pound at a quarter to two. *I* know. Well, you cant afford to lose it. I'll send it to you.

BILL [*his voice and accent suddenly improving*] Not if Aw wiz to stawve for it. Aw aint to be bought.

SHIRLEY. Aint you? Youd sell yourself to the devil for a pint o beer; ony there aint no devil to make the offer.

BILL [*unshamed*] Sao Aw would, mite, and often ev, cheerful. But she cawnt baw me. [*Approaching Barbara*] You wanted maw saoul, did you? Well, you aint got it.

BARBARA. I nearly got it, Bill. But weve sold it back to you for ten thousand pounds.

SHIRLEY. And dear at the money!

BARBARA. No, Peter: it was worth more than money.

BILL [*salvationproof*] It's nao good: you cawnt get rahnd me nah. Aw downt blieve in it; and Awve seen tody that Aw was rawt. [*Going*] Sao long, aol soupkitchener! Ta, ta, Mijor Earl's Grendorter! [*Turning at the gate*] Wot prawce selvytion nah? Snobby Prawce! Ha! ha!

BARBARA [*offering her hand*] Goodbye, Bill.

BILL [*taken aback, half plucks his cap off; then shoves it on again defiantly*] Git aht. [*Barbara drops her hand, discouraged. He has a twinge of remorse*]. But thets aw rawt, you knaow. Nathink pasnl. Naow mellice. Sao long, Judy. [*He goes*].

BARBARA. No malice. So long, Bill.

SHIRLEY [*shaking his head*] You make too much of him, miss, in your innocence.

BARBARA [*going to him*] Peter : I'm like you now. Cleaned out, and lost my job.

SHIRLEY. Youve youth an hope. Thats two better than me.

BARBARA. I'll get you a job, Peter. Thats hope for you : the youth will have to be enough for me. [*She counts her money*]. I have just enough left for two teas at Lockharts, a Rowton doss for you, and my tram and bus home. [*He frowns and rises with offended pride. She takes his arm*]. Dont be proud, Peter : it's sharing between friends. And promise me youll talk to me and not let me cry. [*She draws him towards the gate*].

SHIRLEY. Well, I'm not accustomed to talk to the like of you—

BARBARA [*urgently*] Yes, yes : you must talk to me. Tell me about Tom Paine's books and Bradlaugh's lectures. Come along.

SHIRLEY. Ah, if you would only read Tom Paine in the proper spirit, miss ! [*They go out through the gate together*].

Outside an unpretentious eating-house somewhere between West Ham and London bridge. Customers entering and leaving. The winter evening has fallen and the street lamps are alight. The shops are lighted up. Barbara and Shirley come out.

BARBARA. I must say goodnight now, Peter. Heres your tramfare. I'll walk home.

SHIRLEY. But you cant walk home : youre miles from your home. And youve had nothing in there except a cup of tea. Ive had to eat your food for you. Youve been on your feet all day. You cant walk home on an empty stomach.

BARBARA. If I feel tired I can take a taxi : there is plenty of money at home to pay for it. But I must be alone: I've things to think about. Dont mind my sending you away, Peter: I shall not forget my promise to get you a job.

SHIRLEY. I dont like leaving you. I dont feel that youre fit to be left.

BARBARA. Thank you, dear Peter. But it will be all right: I can take care of myself.

SHIRLEY. I'll bet you can. Better than me. Well, goodnight; and thank you kindly for looking for the job for me. I'll dye my hair this time.

BARBARA. Yes, do, Peter. Goodnight.

They shake hands; and Shirley goes his way. Barbara stands a moment, thinking; then moves off.

A wharf by the riverside. Moonlight. Tide flowing and rivercraft passing. Barbara comes slowly to the brink, and gazes intently at the stream. She takes off her bonnet; looks at it affectionately; kisses it and throws it into the river.

A uniformed watchman hurries in and grips her arm.

WATCHMAN. Now then: whats the game? Ive been watching you. I saw you throw your bonnet into the river. Dont give your mind to throwing yourself after it and giving me the job of fishing you out, because you wont be let do it. [*Shaking her arm*] See?

BARBARA [*smiling wanly*] That is what you thought, is it? Even if I wanted to throw away my own life, Ive no right to risk yours.

The Watchman, startled by her ladylike speech and manner, releases her arm, and steps back respectfully.

WATCHMAN. Youll excuse me, miss; but are you quite yourself this evening?

BARBARA. I'm not at all sure. This morning I was Major Barbara of the Salvation Army in West Ham. Now I'm only Miss Undershaft, of Stevenage House, Wilton Crescent. But you see Ive just drowned Major Barbara; so I suppose I must be Miss Undershaft. Do you think I can find a taxi to take me home? Ive walked a long way, and become quite tired suddenly.

WATCHMAN. There are no taxis about here: the best I can do for you is an ambulance. The ambulance can carry you to the station. They can telephone there to your home for somebody to take charge of you.

BARBARA. Thank you: if youll be so good. I'm quite sane and quite sober; but Ive had a great shock today; and—and— [*she faints into the arms of the watchman*].

WATCHMAN [*saving her from falling*] Steady, miss, steady. [*He eases her down on the flags, and kneels beside her. He blows his whistle three times. He feels her pulse. The ambulance arrives with two bearers, running*].

FIRST BEARER. She's dry.

SECOND BEARER. She's dressed like a Salvation lass. Where's her bonnet?

WATCHMAN. She hasnt been in the water: I stopped her just in time. It's only a faint. She's coming round. Get her to the station as quick as you can. Be civil to her: her people are big West End swells. I'll telephone them. [*They lift Barbara on to the ambulance and carry her off*].

Meanwhile Undershaft and Cusins have spent the evening very differently. The meeting to which they marched has been a great success. Charrington's great hall in the Mile End Road is crowded; and the pavement outside is blocked by people waiting in vain for admission. Two Salvationists come from the hall and set up a huge placard inscribed THE HALL IS FULL. YOU CANNOT COME IN; BUT YOU CAN PRAY FOR US. The people slowly turn away, disappointed.

Inside the hall a combination of Salvation Army bands is accompanying the hymn "Climbing up the Golden Stairs," which the whole congregation is singing with impetuous enthusiasm. The General is standing in front of the platform, in the middle, not singing, but waiting for her turn. Jenny Hill is singing frantically. Cusins, in the middle of the back row, is leading the percussion, Undershaft is vamping a trombone accompaniment.

At the end of the hymn the General raises her hand. Immediately there is dead silence.

THE GENERAL. Friends: we have a duty tonight which we must not forget. God has answered our prayers wonderfully by sending us a great gift: one that will enable us to get through many winters as bitter as this one has been without stinting one of His children of their little ration of bread and milk, or their warm blanket in the shelter. You all know the name of the nobleman who, under God, was the instrument of the first half of that gift. You will pray for him and rejoice in his salvation. You do not know the name of that other generous servant of God who has made up the whole sum for us; and I may not tell it to you. For he is one of those who does not let his right hand know what his left doeth. Friends: he is here among us tonight. [*Tremendous applause*]. This afternoon, when he announced his magnificent offering to me, I exclaimed "Thank God!" He smiled and said "You do not thank me." I told him to come to this meeting and he would hear how we thanked him. He has come; and you have kept my word for me. You may not know him on this side of the grave; but when we cross the river [*with a gesture*]—over there—he will be with us still. And we shall know him by the seal of God on his brow. We will now sing our old favorite "Abide with me."

All rise to begin the hymn. Undershaft steals away from the platform and disappears. Cusins, his drum not being as appropriate to "Abide with me" as it was to the golden stairs, slips out after him.

Both of them make for a greenroom where the tables and chairs and the hooks round the walls are heaped with the coats and wraps and hats of the choir.

Undershaft throws his trombone on the pile of coats on the table, and is mopping his forehead with his handkerchief when Cusins arrives.

UNDERSHAFT. Phui! This is more than I bargained for. I can stand no more of it. [*He snatches up his coat and hat from a chair, and puts them on*]. Come with me to my flat. I have something to say to you.

CUSINS. But I want to call at Wilton Crescent to ask if Barbara has got home safely.

UNDERSHAFT. Never mind Barbara: she can look after herself. Her uniform will protect her better than ten policemen. Come on. It is about Barbara I want to speak to you. [*He hurries out. Cusins has to do likewise*].

In the best room in Undershaft's very comfortable flat in Whitehall Court his valet is placing a tray of drinks on the sideboard. There is a decanter of red wine, and another full of a fluid which deceptively resembles the purest sparkling water. A glowing fire warms the room pleasantly.

Undershaft and Cusins come in, Undershaft pocketing his latchkey.

CUSINS. Nice and warm in here.

UNDERSHAFT [*to the valet, who helps them to get rid of their greatcoats and headgear*] Any messages?

THE VALET. No, sir. Anything to eat, sir?

UNDERSHAFT. No. Something to drink only.

THE VALET. All ready, sir.

UNDERSHAFT [*to Cusins*] It was devilishly cold outside. Try a nip of brandy. Help yourself.

CUSINS. Brandy! Good gracious, no. Lady Britomart is a temperance fanatic. I am allowed nothing stronger than water. [*He pours out a glass of the colorless fluid*]. My throat is horribly dry. I dont know how to sing; and the effect of my attempts at the meetings is to give me incipient laryngitis. [*He swallows a liberal gulp of the fluid*. Aow! [*Choking*] Kkk! What's this? Oh Lord! Red hot firewater. Kkk! Aow! [*He throws what he has left in the glass into the fire, which flames up alarmingly*].

UNDERSHAFT. Take care. You will set the chimney on fire.

CUSINS. It has set my throat on fire. What on earth is it?

UNDERSHAFT. It is only vodka : it wont hurt you.

CUSINS. Give me something cold, for heaven's sake.

UNDERSHAFT [*pouring out a glass of the red wine*] Try my special temperance burgundy.

CUSINS [*swallows the whole glassful greedily*] ! ! !

UNDERSHAFT. Steady ! Steady !

THE VALET. Go easy with that, sir. Mr Undershaft calls it a temperance burgundy ; but I should be sorry to venture on more than one glass of it myself.

CUSINS [*pouring himself out another glass*] Nonsense ! After that fiery stuff it is like milk. [*He empties the glass*]. Ah ! that's better.

UNDERSHAFT. Are you all right now ?

CUSINS. Perfectly.

UNDERSHAFT. Good. By the way, you wont mind my getting rid of this. [*He takes the S brooch from his collar and throws it on the table*].

CUSINS. That means you are getting rid of Barbara.

UNDERSHAFT. Not at all.

CUSINS. Yes. She has refused to swallow Bodger's whisky. Do you think she is any more likely to swallow your money and gunpowder ?

UNDERSHAFT. She has swallowed a good deal of it already, my friend. What do you suppose she has been living on all these years ?

CUSINS. You think you will end by making us swallow them.

UNDERSHAFT. We all have to swallow them. There are mystical powers above and behind the three of us that will make short work of your scruples.

CUSINS [*somewhat aggressively. He is no longer sober*] Do you think I dont know all about the mystical powers, Machiavelli ? You remember what Euripides says about your money and gunpowder ?

UNDERSHAFT. No. Does he mention me ?

CUSINS [*declaiming*]

One and another
In money and guns may outpass his brother ;
And men in their millions float and flow
And seethe with a million hopes as leaven ;
And they win their will or they miss their will ;
And their hopes are dead or are pined for still ;
But whoe'er can know
As the long days go
That to live is happy, has found his heaven.

Colloquially] My translation. What do you think of it?

UNDERSHAFT. I think, my friend, that if you wish to know, as the long days go, that to live is happy, you must first acquire money enough for a decent life, and power enough to be your own master.

CUSINS. You are damnably discouraging. [*Again declaiming*]

It is so hard a thing to see
That the spirit of God, whate'er it be,
The Law that abides and changes not, ages long,
The Eternal and Nature-born : these things be strong ?
What else is Wisdom ? What of Man's endeavour,
Or God's high grace, so lovely and so great ?
To stand from fear set free ?
To breathe and wait ?
To hold a hand uplifted over Fate ?
And shall not Barbara be loved for ever ?

UNDERSHAFT. Euripides mentions Barbara, does he ?

CUSINS. It is a fair translation. The word means loveliness.

UNDERSHAFT. May I ask, as Barbara's father, how much a year she is to be loved for ever on ?

CUSINS. As Barbara's father, that is more your affair than mine. I can feed her by teaching Greek : that is about all.

UNDERSHAFT. Do you consider it a good match for her ?

CUSINS [*with polite obstinacy*] Mr Undershaft : when I am sober I am in many ways a weak, timid, ineffectual person ; and my health is far from satisfactory. At present I am very far from sober, thanks to your Intemperance Burgundy. But, drunk or sober, whenever I feel that I must have anything, I get it, sooner or later. I feel that way about Barbara. I dont like marriage; I feel intensely afraid of it; and I don't know what I shall do with Barbara or what she will do with me; but I feel that I and nobody else must marry her. Please regard that as settled. Not that I wish to be arbitrary; but why should I waste your time in discussing what is inevitable?

UNDERSHAFT. You mean that you will stick at nothing, not even the conversion of the Salvation Army to the worship of Dionysos.

CUSINS. The business of the Salvation Army is to save, not to wrangle about the name of the Pathfinder. Dionysos or another: what does it matter?

UNDERSHAFT [*taking Cusins affectionately by the shoulders*] Professor Cusins: you are a young man after my own heart.

CUSINS [*returning his embrace*] Mr Undershaft: you are, as far as I am able to gather, a most infernal old rascal; but you appeal very strongly to my sense of ironic humor.

UNDERSHAFT. Good. We shall get on very well together. Have you ever thought of going into business? My business: money and gunpowder? Barbara's money will come from it. Why not help to earn it? Have you thought of that at all?

CUSINS. Look here, Machiavelli: I am interested in thought reading, and have, in fact, made some experiments in it. But I object to your trying it on me. When my head is clear I will tell you exactly what I think. Just at present I am delightfully drunk and happy. And the room is very hot. Might we have the window open for a moment?

UNDERSHAFT. Certainly. [*Calling*] James! I should like a breath of fresh air myself. [*To the Valet, who has come forward*] Draw back those curtains; and open the window, will you?

THE VALET [*doubtfully*] It's a very windy night, sir.

UNDERSHAFT. So much the better. It's only for a minute to freshen the room.

The Valet draws the curtains apart and opens the window, which has no sash, and opens like double doors. The wind rushes in.

CUSINS [*inhaling a full breath*] Oh, what a relief! [*He reels*]. Hullo! Wha's ma'er? Room's going round.

UNDERSHAFT [*holding him up*] Steady, man, steady.

CUSINS. Wha's 'appening? The waves, the waves. How d'we get on ship? [*Undershaft saves him from falling*]. Stea'y, Macklevelly, stea'y. Ha! ha! ha! Fernal ole laskl; buppeal velly slongly my sense of ile—ile—ile— [*with a supreme effort to say it*] ilonnic humor. Ha! ha! ha! ha! O ha! ha! ha! ha! ha!

UNDERSHAFT [*to the Valet*] Lend a hand, will you?

THE VALET. Right, sir.

UNDERSHAFT. Get his feet on the rug: the floor's like wax.

CUSINS [*quoting The Frogs, by Aristophanes*] Brekekekex co-ax co-ax. Brekekekex co-ax.

THE VALET. What's he trying to say, sir?

UNDERSHAFT. Greek, I expect. Come come, Euripides! Pull yourself together.

CUSINS. No, no, no. 'Sglaceful. Not Ulipplees, Allisloffnes. Brekklekkex co-ax co-ax co— [*Calling*] Steward! [*Looking at the Valet*] Oh, there you are, steward. Ole man dlunk, bline dlunk. Purrimabed. [*Sentimentally*] Be kind to him, steward. Gooni' o' man. Gooni', S'eward. Gooni'. Ni, ni [*he falls fast asleep; and they have to let him down flat on the floor*].

UNDERSHAFT. What the deuce are we to do with him?

THE VALET [*dubiously*] I am afraid he's here for the night, sir.

They carry him to bed.

The dining room at Wilton Crescent next morning. Breakfast is ready. Morrison in attendance. Lady Britomart comes in.

LADY BRITOMART. Nobody down yet!

MORRISON. No, my lady.

LADY BRITOMART. Miss Barbara has gone, I suppose.

MORRISON. No, my lady. Miss Barbara is not up yet.

LADY BRITOMART. What! Are you sure?

MORRISON. Quite sure, my lady. Miss Barbara came in late last night and said she was not to be called.

LADY BRITOMART. Not to be called!!!

MORRISON. Yes, my lady. She said she was very tired and must have twelve hours sleep.

LADY BRITOMART. Was she quite well?

MORRISON. A little pale, my lady, and without her bonnet. I hadnt much time to notice; for she went straight upstairs, and left me to settle with the taxi and the policeman.

LADY BRITOMART. Policeman! What are you talking about, Morrison?

MORRISON. He came with her in the taxi. He asked questions, my lady. Was she Miss Undershaft? Was it all right? And an account to settle for the taxi, and for an ambulance, and some tea at the police station. I thought it best to pay and say nothing.

LADY BRITOMART. An ambulance! There must have been some accident. You are quite sure she was not hurt?

MORRISON. She seemed all right, my lady.

LADY BRITOMART. But you say she was brought home by a policeman.

MORRISON. I think he wanted to make sure who she was: whether he had her name and address all right, as it were.

LADY BRITOMART. Hm! What have you laid all those covers for? Have the young ladies invited anyone to breakfast?

MORRISON. You are expecting Mr Cusins and Mr Lomax, my lady. The car is ordered for half-past ten to take the party to—to—to—

LADY BRITOMART. Well? To where?

MORRISON. To Mr Undershaft's premises, I think, my lady.

LADY BRITOMART. To the factory, you mean?

MORRISON [*apologetically*] Well, yes, my lady.

LADY BRITOMART. The factory pays your wages, Morrison.

MORRISON. Yes, my lady. That is what factories are for.

We must put up with them. Bacon and eggs, my lady, as usual?

LADY BRITOMART. No: I'll have a sausage this morning.

Morrison serves the sausage. Lomax comes in.

LADY BRITOMART. You are late, Charles. Where is Adolphus?

LOMAX [*taking a seat at the table*] He will be here soon. He was out all night. He wasnt quite himself when he came home. [*To Morrison*] Eggs and bacon, please. [*He is served*].

LADY BRITOMART. When you say he wasnt quite himself, Charles, what exactly do you mean?

Cusins enters, in an ordinary lounge suit.

LADY BRITOMART. Good morning, Adolphus. Charles was just telling me that when you came home this morning you were not quite yourself. May I ask what was the matter with you?

CUSINS [*taking his seat at the table*] Only a hangover. [*To Morrison*] Coffee, please. Nothing to eat. [*To Lady Britomart*] I got blind drunk last night.

LADY BRITOMART. Blind drunk!!!

CUSINS. I went home with your husband. Have you ever tasted vodka, Lady Brit.?

LADY BRITOMART. Certainly not.

CUSINS. It looks exactly like spring water. The strongest spirits taste like milk after it.

Sarah bounces in, fresh from her morning toilet.

SARAH. Good morning. [*She kisses her mother, then kisses Lomax*]. Morning, Dolly. [*To Morrison*] Buttermilk and kippers, please. [*She sits*].

CUSINS. A new Spanish burgundy, warranted free from added alcohol: a Temperance burgundy in fact, finished me. Its richness in natural alcohol made any addition superfluous.

LOMAX. You know, there is a certain amount of tosh about alcohol. Burgundy is either burgundy or it isnt. If it is, it's hot stuff unless you are used to it.

CUSINS. Quite true. Ive never been really drunk before. I rather liked it last night. I regret it now.

Barbara comes in, in ordinary dress, black and simple, contrasting with Sarah.

BARBARA. Good morning everybody. [*To Morrison*] Porridge: lots of porridge. And grape fruit. I'm as hungry as a hunter.

LOMAX. Oh, I say! Youve chucked the uniform.

LADY BRITOMART. You mean that Barbara has changed her dress, Charles. Why not say so?

LOMAX. No: I'm afraid I mean something more than that. I mean she has chucked her salvation things.

BARBARA. Cholly means exactly what he says, mother. We are all going to the factory of money and gunpowder, death and destruction, on which we are living. The uniform would be out of place there. Tell us about the meeting, Dolly.

CUSINS. It was an amazing meeting. We prayed for Bodger: it was most touching. Then we prayed for the anonymous donor of the £5000. Your father would not let his name be given.

LOMAX. That was rather fine of the old man, you know. Most chaps would have wanted the advertisement.

CUSINS. He said all the charitable institutions would be down on him like vultures on a battlefield if he gave his name.

LADY BRITOMART. That is Andrew all over. He never does a proper thing without giving an improper reason for it.

CUSINS. I cant blame him. All my life Ive been doing improper things for proper reasons.

BARBARA. Tell me the truth, Dolly. Were you really ever in earnest about the Army? Would you have joined if you had never seen me?

CUSINS. Well—er— Well, possibly as a collector of religions—

LOMAX. Not as a drummer though. You know, Dolly, you are a very clearheaded brainy chap; and you must have felt what even I feel, that there is a certain amount of tosh about the Salvation Army. Now the claims of the Church of England—

LADY BRITOMART. Thats enough, Charles. Speak of something suited to your mental capacity.

LOMAX. But surely the Church of England is suited to all our capacities.

LADY BRITOMART. That is its worst fault: a thoroughly English one.

LOMAX. You are so awfully strongminded, Lady Brit.

LADY BRITOMART. Dont dare to say so. If there is one thing in the world that I am not, it is a strongminded woman.

Morrison returns.

LADY BRITOMART. What is it?

MORRISON. Mr Undershaft has just drove up to the door, my lady.

LADY BRITOMART. Well, let him in.

MORRISON. Shall I announce him, my lady? or is he at home here in a manner of speaking?

LADY BRITOMART. That is a very difficult question, Morrison. What do you advise, Adolphus? You are his friend: you got drunk with him.

CUSINS. I did not marry him. I tolerate him because he was the instrument of Barbara's birth; but to me he is the Prince of Darkness.

LADY BRITOMART. You are getting drunker and drunker, Adolphus. Finish your breakfast and stop talking.

LOMAX. Has the old man a latchkey?

LADY BRITOMART. Another word, Charles; and I'll box your ears. What do you say, Sarah?

SARAH. As Morrison has raised the question I should leave him to solve it.

BARBARA. Of course: Morrison knows better than anybody. Dont you, Morrison?

MORRISON. Well, miss, the occasion is new to me. But as he has not come to breakfast, I could shew him into the library with your ladyship's leave.

LADY BRITOMART. Yes, do, Morrison.

Morrison goes.

LADY BRITOMART. Children: go and get ready.

BARBARA. Ive not finished my porridge.

LADY BRITOMART. Take it with you.

Barbara does so and goes out with Sarah.

LADY BRITOMART. Charles: tell Stephen to come to the

library in five minutes or so.

LOMAX. Righto. [*He goes*].

LADY BRITOMART. I wish Charles would not say righto: we shall have Morrison saying it next. Adolphus: are you sober enough to tell them to send round the carriage in fifteen minutes?

CUSINS [*rising*] I will try. I will take an emetic, I think.

LADY BRITOMART. Do, Adolphus: do.

He goes.

Meanwhile Morrison has gone down the grand stairs to the entrance hall and opened the hall door. Undershaft comes in.

UNDERSHAFT. Morning, Morrison. You quite well, eh?

MORRISON [*taking Undershaft's overcoat and hat*] Quite well, thank you, sir. Glad to see you home again, sir.

UNDERSHAFT. Home again? Hm! You are more at home here than I am by this time, eh?

MORRISON. Oh, I am only part of the house, sir.

UNDERSHAFT. Where is her ladyship?

MORRISON. In the library, sir.

UNDERSHAFT. I forget where the library is. Which door?

MORRISON. Where you were the night before last, sir. Shall I shew you?

UNDERSHAFT [*following him*] Yes, yes. I am only a visitor here.

Morrison leads the way upstairs to the library.

MORRISON. I will tell her ladyship, sir. [*He closes the library door, leaving Undershaft alone*].

Undershaft examines the room like a stranger, making faces expressive of strong distaste. He hates the place.

Lady Britomart bounces in. Undershaft clears his countenance, and puts on his best husbandly manner.

UNDERSHAFT. Good morning, dear. How fortunate to find you alone!

LADY BRITOMART. Dont be sentimental, Andrew. Sit down.

They sit side by side on the settee.

LADY BRITOMART [*attacking instantly*] Sarah must have £800 a year until Charles Lomax comes into his property. Barbara will need more, especially if she has a lot of children ; and she will need it permanently, because Adolphus is only a professor and hasnt any property.

UNDERSHAFT [*resignedly*] Yes, my dear : I will see to it. Anything else ? for yourself, for instance ?

LADY BRITOMART. I want to talk to you about Stephen.

UNDERSHAFT [*rather wearily*] Dont, my dear. Stephen doesnt interest me.

LADY BRITOMART. He does interest me. He is our son.

UNDERSHAFT. Do you really think so ? He has induced us to bring him into the world ; but he chose his parents very incongruously, I think. I see nothing of myself in him, and less of you.

LADY BRITOMART. Andrew : Stephen is an excellent son, and a most steady, capable, highminded young man. You are simply trying to find an excuse for disinheriting him.

UNDERSHAFT. My dear Biddy : the Undershaft tradition disinherits him. It would be dishonest of me to leave the cannon foundry to my son.

LADY BRITOMART. It would be most unnatural and improper of you to leave it to anyone else, Andrew. Do you suppose this wicked and immoral tradition can be kept up for ever ? Do you pretend that Stephen could not carry on the foundry just as well as all the other sons of the big business houses ?

UNDERSHAFT. Yes : he could learn the office routine without understanding the business, like all the other sons ; and the firm would go on by its own momentum until the real Undershaft—probably an Italian or a German—would invent something new, and cut him out.

LADY BRITOMART. There is nothing that any Italian or German could do that Stephen could not do. And Stephen at least has breeding.

UNDERSHAFT. The son of a foundling ! Nonsense !

LADY BRITOMART. My son, Andrew ! And even you may have good blood in your veins for all you know.

UNDERSHAFT. True. Probably I have. That is another argument in favor of a foundling.

LADY BRITOMART. Andrew : dont be aggravating. And

dont be wicked. At present you are both.

UNDERSHAFT. This conversation is part of the Undershaft tradition, Biddy. Every Undershaft's wife has treated him to it ever since the house was founded. It is mere waste of breath. If the tradition be ever broken it will be for an abler man than Stephen.

LADY BRITOMART [*pouting*] Then go away.

UNDERSHAFT [*deprecatory*] Go away !

LADY BRITOMART. Yes : go away. If you will do nothing for Stephen, you are not wanted here. Go to your foundling, whoever he is ; and look after him.

UNDERSHAFT. The fact is, Biddy—

LADY BRITOMART. Dont call me Biddy. I dont call you Andy.

UNDERSHAFT. I will not call my wife Britomart : it is not good sense. Seriously, my love, the Undershaft tradition has landed me in a difficulty. I am getting on in years ; and my partner Lazarus has at last made a stand and insisted that the succession must be settled one way or the other. Of course he is quite right. But I havnt found a fit successor yet.

LADY BRITOMART [*obstinately*] There is Stephen.

UNDERSHAFT. Thats just it : all the foundlings I can find are exactly like Stephen.

LADY BRITOMART. Andrew ! !

UNDERSHAFT. I want a man with no relations and no schooling : that is, a man who would be out of the running altogether if he were not a strong man. And I cant find him. Every blessed foundling nowadays is snapped up in his infancy by Barnardo homes, or School Board officers, or Boards of Guardians ; and if he shews the least ability he is fastened on by schoolmasters ; trained to win scholarships like a racehorse ; crammed with secondhand ideas ; drilled and disciplined in docility and what they call good taste ; and lamed for life. If you want to keep the foundry in the family, you had better find an eligible foundling and marry him to Barbara.

LADY BRITOMART. Ah ! Barbara ! Your pet ! You would sacrifice Stephen to Barbara.

UNDERSHAFT. Cheerfully. And you, my dear, would boil Barbara to make soup for Stephen.

LADY BRITOMART. Andrew : this is not a question of our likings and dislikings : it is a question of duty. It is your duty to make Stephen your successor.

UNDERSHAFT. Just as much as it is your duty to submit to your husband. Come, Biddy ! these tricks of the governing class dont go down with me. I am one of the governing class myself ; and it is waste of time giving tracts to a missionary. I have the power in this matter ; and I am not to be humbugged into using it for your purposes.

LADY BRITOMART. Andrew : you can talk my head off ; but you cant change wrong into right. And your tie is all on one side. Put it straight.

UNDERSHAFT [*disconcerted*] It wont stay unless it's pinned [*he fumbles at it with childish grimaces*]—

Stephen comes in.

STEPHEN [*at the door*] I beg your pardon [*about to retire*].

LADY BRITOMART. No : come in, Stephen. [*Stephen comes forward to his mother's writing table*].

UNDERSHAFT [*not very cordially*] Good morning.

STEPHEN [*coldly*] Good morning.

UNDERSHAFT [*to Lady Britomart*] He knows all about the tradition, I suppose ?

LADY BRITOMART. Yes. [*To Stephen*]. It is what I told you last night, Stephen.

UNDERSHAFT [*sulkily*] I understand you want to come into the cannon business.

STEPHEN. *I* go into trade ! Certainly not.

UNDERSHAFT [*opening his eyes, greatly eased in mind and manner*] Oh ! in that case—

LADY BRITOMART. Cannons are not trade, Stephen. They are enterprise.

STEPHEN. I have no intention of becoming a man of business in any sense. I have no capacity for business and no taste for it. I intend to devote myself to politics.

UNDERSHAFT [*rising*] My dear boy : this is an immense relief to me. And I trust it may prove an equally good thing for the country. I was afraid you would consider yourself disparaged and slighted. [*He moves towards Stephen as if to shake hands with him*].

LADY BRITOMART [*rising and interposing*] Stephen: I cannot allow you to throw away an enormous property like this.

STEPHEN [*stiffly*] Mother: there must be an end to treating me as a child, if you please. [*Lady Britomart recoils, deeply wounded by his tone*]. Until last night I did not take your attitude seriously, because I did not think you meant it seriously. But I find now that you left me in the dark as to matters which you should have explained to me years ago. I am extremely hurt and offended. Any further discussion of my intentions had better take place with my father, as between one man and another.

LADY BRITOMART. Stephen! [*She sits down again, her eyes filling with tears*].

UNDERSHAFT [*with grave compassion*] You see, my dear, it is only the big men who can be treated as children.

STEPHEN. I am sorry, mother, that you have forced me—

UNDERSHAFT [*stopping him*] Yes, yes, yes, yes: thats all right, Stephen. She wont interfere with you any more: your independence is achieved: you have won your latchkey. Dont rub it in; and above all, dont apologize. [*He resumes his seat*]. Now what about your future, as between one man and another—I beg your pardon, Biddy: as between two men and a woman.

LADY BRITOMART [*who has pulled herself together strongly*] I quite understand, Stephen. By all means go your own way if you feel strong enough. [*Stephen sits down magisterially in the chair at the writing table with an air of affirming his majority*].

UNDERSHAFT. It is settled that you do not ask for the succession to the cannon business.

STEPHEN. I hope it is settled that I repudiate the cannon business.

UNDERSHAFT. Come, come! dont be so devilishly sulky: it's boyish. Freedom should be generous. Besides,

I owe you a fair start in life in exchange for disinheriting you. You cant become prime minister all at once. Havnt you a turn for something? What about literature, art, and so forth?

STEPHEN. I have nothing of the artist about me, either in faculty or character, thank Heaven!

UNDERSHAFT. A philosopher, perhaps? Eh?

STEPHEN. I make no such ridiculous pretension.

UNDERSHAFT. Just so. Well, there is the army, the navy, the Church, the Bar. The Bar requires some ability. What about the Bar?

STEPHEN. I have not studied law. And I am afraid I have not the necessary push—I believe that is the name barristers give to their vulgarity—for success in pleading.

UNDERSHAFT. Rather a difficult case, Stephen. Hardly anything left but the stage, is there? [*Stephen makes an impatient movement*]. Well, come! is there anything you know or care for?

STEPHEN [*rising and looking at him steadily*] I know the difference between right and wrong.

UNDERSHAFT [*hugely tickled*] You dont say so! What! no capacity for business, no knowledge of law, no sympathy with art, no pretension to philosophy; only a simple knowledge of the secret that has puzzled all the philosophers, baffled all the lawyers, muddled all the men of business, and ruined most of the artists: the secret of right and wrong. Why, man, youre a genius, a master of masters, a god! At twentyfour, too!

STEPHEN [*keeping his temper with difficulty*] You are pleased to be facetious. I pretend to nothing more than any honorable English gentleman claims as his birthright [*he sits down angrily*].

UNDERSHAFT. Oh, thats everybody's birthright. Look at poor little Jenny Hill, the Salvation lassie! she would think you were laughing at her if you asked her to stand up in the street and teach grammar or geography or mathematics or even drawing room dancing; but it never occurs to her to doubt that she can teach morals and religion. You are all alike, you respectable people.

You cant tell me the bursting strain of a ten-inch gun, which is a very simple matter ; but you all think you can tell me the bursting strain of a man under temptation. You darent handle high explosives ; but youre all ready to handle honesty and truth and justice and the whole duty of man, and kill one another at that game. What a country ! What a world !

LADY BRITOMART [*uneasily*] What do you think he had better do, Andrew ?

UNDERSHAFT. Oh, just what he wants to do. He knows nothing and he thinks he knows everything. That points clearly to a political career. Get him a private secretaryship to someone who can get him an Under Secretaryship ; and then leave him alone. He will find his natural and proper place in the end on the Treasury Bench.

STEPHEN [*springing up again*] I am sorry, sir, that you force me to forget the respect due to you as my father. I am an Englishman and I will not hear the Government of my country insulted. [*He thrusts his hands in his pockets, and walks angrily across to the window*].

UNDERSHAFT [*with a touch of brutality*] The government of your country ! *I* am the government of your country : I, and Lazarus. Do you suppose that you and half a dozen amateurs like you, sitting in a row in that foolish gabble shop, can govern Undershaft and Lazarus ? No, my friend : you will do what pays us. You will make war when it suits us, and keep peace when it doesnt. You will find out that trade requires certain measures when we have decided on those measures. When I want anything to keep my dividends up, you will discover that my want is a national need. When other people want something to keep my dividends down, you will call out the police and military. And in return you shall have the support and applause of my newspapers, and the delight of imagining that you are a great statesman. Government of your country ! Be off with you, my boy, and play with your caucuses and leading articles and historic parties and great leaders and burning questions and the rest of your toys. *I* am going back to my counting-house to pay the piper and call the tune.

STEPHEN [*actually smiling, and putting his hand on his father's shoulder with indulgent patronage*] Really, my dear father, it is impossible to be angry with you. You dont know how absurd all this sounds to me. You are very properly proud of having been industrious enough to make money ; and it is greatly to your credit that you have made so much of it. But it has kept you in circles where you are valued for your money and deferred to for it, instead of in the doubtless very old-fashioned and behind-the-times public school and university where I formed my habits of mind. It is natural for you to think that money governs England ; but you must allow me to think I know better.

UNDERSHAFT. And what does govern England, pray ?

STEPHEN. Character, father, character.

UNDERSHAFT. Whose character ? Yours or mine ?

STEPHEN. Neither yours nor mine, father, but the best elements in the English national character.

UNDERSHAFT. Stephen : Ive found your profession for you. Youre a born journalist. I'll start you with a high-toned weekly review. There !

Before Stephen can reply Sarah, Barbara, Lomax, and Cusins come in ready for walking. Barbara crosses the room to the window and looks out. Cusins drifts amiably to the armchair. Lomax remains near the door, whilst Sarah comes to her mother.

Stephen goes to the smaller writing table and busies himself with his letters.

SARAH. Go and get ready, mamma : the car is waiting.

Lady Britomart leaves the room.

UNDERSHAFT [*to Sarah*] Good day, my dear. Good morning, Mr Lomax.

LOMAX [*vaguely*] Ahdedoo.

UNDERSHAFT [*to Cusins*] Quite well after last night, Euripides, eh ?

CUSINS. As well as can be expected.

UNDERSHAFT. Thats right. [*To Barbara*] So you are coming to see my death and devastation factory, Barbara?

BARBARA [*at the window*] You came yesterday to see my salvation factory. I promised you a return visit.

LOMAX [*coming forward between Sarah and Undershaft*] Youll find it awfully interesting. Ive been through the Woolwich Arsenal; and it gives you a ripping feeling of security, you know, to think of the lot of beggars we could kill if it came to fighting. [*To Undershaft, with sudden solemnity*] Still, it must be rather an awful reflection for you, from the religious point of view as it were. Youre getting on, you know, and all that.

SARAH. You dont mind Cholly, papa, do you?

LOMAX [*much taken aback*] Oh I say!

UNDERSHAFT. Mr Lomax looks at the matter in a very proper spirit, my dear.

LOMAX. Just so. Thats all I meant, I assure you.

SARAH. Are you coming, Stephen?

STEPHEN. Well, I am rather busy—er— [*Magnanimously*] Oh well, yes: I'll come. That is, if there is room for me.

UNDERSHAFT. I can take two with me in a little motor I am experimenting with for field use. You wont mind its being rather unfashionable. It's not painted yet; but it's bullet proof.

LOMAX [*appalled at the prospect of confronting Wilton Crescent in an unpainted motor*] Oh I say!

SARAH. Our own car for me, thank you. Barbara doesnt mind what she's seen in.

LOMAX. I say, Dolly, old chap: do you really mind the car being a guy? Because of course if you do I'll go in it. Still—

CUSINS. I prefer it.

LOMAX. Thanks awfully, old man. Come, my ownest. [*He hurries out. Sarah follows him*].

CUSINS [*moodily walking across to Lady Britomart's writing table*] Why are we two coming to this Works Department of Hell? that is what I ask myself.

BARBARA. I have always thought of it as a sort of pit where lost creatures with blackened faces stirred up smoky fires and were driven and tormented by my father. Is it like that, dad?

UNDERSHAFT [*scandalized*] My dear! It is a spotlessly clean and beautiful hillside town.

CUSINS. With a Methodist chapel? Oh do say theres a Methodist chapel.

UNDERSHAFT. There are several, all of different persuasions. My men are all strongly religious. In the High Explosives Sheds they object to the presence of Agnostics as unsafe.

BARBARA. And yet they obey all your orders?

UNDERSHAFT. I never give them any orders. When I speak to one of them it is "Well, Jones, is the baby doing well? and has Mrs Jones made a good recovery?" "Nicely, thank you, sir." And thats all.

CUSINS. But Jones has to be kept in order. How do you maintain discipline among your men?

UNDERSHAFT. I dont. They do. You see, the one thing Jones wont stand is any rebellion from the man under him, or any assertion of social equality between the wife of the man with 4 shillings a week less than himself, and Mrs Jones! Of course they all rebel against me, theoretically. Practically, every man of them keeps the man just below him in his place. I never meddle with them. I never bully them. I dont even bully Lazarus. I say that certain things are to be done; but I dont order anybody to do them. I dont say, mind you, that there is no ordering about and snubbing and even bullying. The men snub the boys and order them about; the carmen snub the sweepers; the artisans snub the unskilled laborers; the foremen drive and bully both the laborers and artisans; the assistant engineers find fault with the foremen; the chief engineers drop on the assistants; the departmental managers worry the chiefs; and the clerks have tall hats and hymnbooks and keep up the social tone by refusing to associate on equal terms with anybody. The result is a considerable profit, some of which is spent in this house.

CUSINS [*revolted*] You really are a—well, what I was saying yesterday.

BARBARA. What was he saying yesterday?

UNDERSHAFT. Never mind, my dear. He thinks I have made you unhappy. Have I?

BARBARA. Do you think I can be happy in this vulgar silly dress? I! who have worn the uniform. Do you understand what you have done to me? Yesterday I had a man's soul in my hand. I set him in the way of life with his face to salvation. But when we took your money he turned back to drunkenness and derision. [*With intense conviction*] I will never forgive you that. If I had a child, and you destroyed its body with your explosives—if you murdered Dolly with your horrible guns—I could forgive you if my forgiveness would open the gates of heaven to you. But to take a human soul from me, and turn it into the soul of a wolf! that is worse than any murder.

UNDERSHAFT. Does my daughter despair so easily? Can you strike a man to the heart and leave no mark on him?

BARBARA [*her face lighting up*] Oh, you are right: he can never be lost now: where was my faith?

CUSINS. Oh, clever clever devil!

BARBARA. You may be a devil; but God speaks through you sometimes. [*She takes her father's hands and kisses them*]. You have given me back my happiness: I feel it deep down now, though my spirit is troubled.

UNDERSHAFT. You have learnt something. That always feels at first as if you had lost something.

BARBARA. Well, take me to the factory of death; and let me learn something more. There must be some truth or other behind all this frightful irony. Come, Dolly. [*She goes out*].

CUSINS. My guardian angel! [*To Undershaft*] Avaunt! [*He follows Barbara*].

STEPHEN [*quietly, at the writing table*] You must not mind Cusins, father. He is a very amiable good fellow; but he is a Greek scholar and naturally a little eccentric.

UNDERSHAFT. Ah, quite so. Thank you, Stephen. Thank you. [*He goes out*].

Stephen smiles patronizingly; buttons his coat responsibly; and crosses the room to the door. Lady Britomart, dressed for out-of-doors, opens it before he reaches it. She looks round for the others; looks at Stephen; and turns to go without a word.

STEPHEN [*embarrassed*] Mother–

LADY BRITOMART. Dont be apologetic, Stephen. And dont forget that you have outgrown your mother. [*She goes out*].

The entrance hall. They all come downstairs in the order in which they left the library. Morrison is waiting for them; and nothing is said while the men get into their overcoats and hats, with Morrison helping Undershaft. When they are all ready Morrison opens the door and finds an armored car waiting.

MORRISON [*authoritatively*] Higher up, please, higher up. You cant park yourself here.

UNDERSHAFT. All right, all right. That is my car, Morrison.

MORRISON. I beg your pardon, sir.

UNDERSHAFT. Room for two besides myself. My dear—

LADY BRITOMART. Most certainly not. I go in my own car. Take Barbara and Adolphus: they are accustomed to disreputable conveyances.

UNDERSHAFT. Can you drive a car, Mr Lomax?

LOMAX. Ra-therrr.

LADY BRITOMART. Andrew: have you no regard for your children's lives? His licence was endorsed last week for driving to the public danger with his arm round Sarah.

LOMAX. But I assure you I can drive quite safely with one hand.

LADY BRITOMART. Possibly. But you cannot see your way safely through the traffic in Knightsbridge while you are kissing Sarah. The magistrate said so; and I agree with the magistrate. You and Sarah will come in my car; and I shall sit between you. Stephen will sit in front. Now dont dawdle.

Sarah, Lomax and Stephen obediently hurry out.

LADY BRITOMART. The military lorry will have to shew us the way—unless you two are frozen to death in it. [*She goes out*].

UNDERSHAFT [*to Barbara*] It is not a military lorry, my dear. You will be quite comfortable.

Barbara and Adolphus go out.

UNDERSHAFT [*following*] Good morning, Morrison.

MORRISON. Shall we see you again this evening, sir ? I have your room ready for you, sir.

UNDERSHAFT [*dashing out*] No, by George ! Goodbye.

MORRISON [*regretfully*] Goodbyc, sir.

Left alone, Morrison shuts the door and throws off his professional manner. He shakes his head over the unfortunate domestic incompatibility of thc heads of the household ; then takes a newspaper from the hall table, and goes off to have an easy time in his own quarters.

A road skirting a green hill, up the opposite slopes of which, parallel to the road, runs what appears to be a white wall, ending at the top in a tower with steps winding up it spirally. In enormous black letters on the white wall are the names UNDERSHAFT up one side and LAZARUS down the other.

Along the road come Undershaft's armored car followed by Lady Britomart's limousine. The limousine stops, honking violently. The armored car stops. The occupants alight, except Lady Britomart.

UNDERSHAFT. What is the matter ? Have you broken down?

LOMAX [*who has a camera in his hand*] Sorry to stop you ; but Sarah wants a photograph of your shop front.

BARBARA. So do I. I shall send it to the Society for saving our countryside from disfiguring advertisements. This is the whited wall in the Bible. How could you spoil that hill with it merely to flaunt your name on it ?

LADY BRITOMART [*putting her head out of the window of the limousine*] You must have all that knocked down and taken away instantly, Andrew. I will not have our name daubed all over the home counties.

UNDERSHAFT. They are not walls, my love. They are the chimneys of my smelting works. When they are swept twice a year we get some tons of silver out of the soot, which is quite clean and white. The name of the firm can be read for ten miles with a good glass : it is one of the sights of the county. People feel as Sarah does that they must photograph it. For twenty square miles you cannot escape from it. The advertisement is worth several thousands a year to us, and, incidentally, my dear, to you.

LADY BRITOMART. In short, you did it for our sakes.

UNDERSHAFT. No : for the sake of the firm. Everything is for the sake of the firm here.

LOMAX. Sort of Totalitarian State, what ?

UNDERSHAFT. Precisely, Mr Lomax.

LADY BRITOMART. Monstrous. [*She disappears into the limousine*].

SARAH. Was Lazarus a foundling, papa ? Why did they give him a Jewish name ?

UNDERSHAFT. Oh no. The Undershafts are the foundlings. It is part of the tradition that they should take a partner with a Jewish name. It suggests financial ability ; and he gets all the blame when our profits are considered exorbitant.

CUSINS. A scapegoat, then ?

UNDERSHAFT. Exactly : a scapegoat.

CUSINS. That is the role of the Jew in modern Capitalism.

UNDERSHAFT. Yes ; but it was an Undershaft invention. Most of these notions are.

LADY BRITOMART [*reappearing*] If you dont drive on I will get out and walk. I will not sit here listening to Andrew glorying in his wickedness.

Her children scramble back to their cars.

LOMAX. Righto ! [*He gets in*].

CUSINS [*with one foot on the step of the armored car*] I must allow myself to point out, Machiavelli, that the adoption plan is not only an Undershaft tradition : it is a Japanese custom. [*He gets in*].

UNDERSHAFT. It is a very sensible one. We have a Japanese

temple in the village. The Shinto religion suits us exactly. I, of course, am its Mikado. [*He gets in*].

The cars move off, and arrive presently at the works of Undershaft and Lazarus in a forest of cranes and huge tubular metal structures of one sort or another. Factory and office buildings all about.

Undershaft and his family alight with their betrotheds, and stare about them at the labyrinth of buildings and monster tubes.

LADY BRITOMART. I refuse to walk another step through all these sheds and pipes and boilers. They mean nothing to me. I have never asked you to come and look at the kitchen range and the scullery sink. Why is that roof making noises like a whale with asthma ?

UNDERSHAFT. It is breathing, my love.

LADY BRITOMART. What is it breathing ?

UNDERSHAFT. Just what you are breathing. Common air.

LOMAX. Arent you overdoing this ventilation business a bit ? Sarah inherits that from you : she is crazy on open windows. I am always telling her that there is a certain amount of tosh about fresh air. I say shut your windows and stop blowing your nose.

SARAH. Shut up, Cholly. A handkerchief lasts me a week : it lasts you half a day.

LADY BRITOMART. You have been brought up stuffily, Charles. My daughters are fresh air girls. I hope Andrew appreciates that fact.

UNDERSHAFT. Come in and see what this shed does with the air it breathes. It is worth seeing.

They go into the shed, Cusins bringing up the rear with Undershaft.

CUSINS. Nitrogen from the air, I suppose ?

UNDERSHAFT. Yes. Salts of ammonia.

They follow the others in.

The interior of the shed is like a scene in a pantomime representing a Snow King's cave. It rains sulphate of ammonia.

LADY BRITOMART. This is ridiculous. Is it snow, or salt, or what ?

CUSINS. Nitrates to make explosives.

UNDERSHAFT. Or sulphates to fertilize the fields your farmers are exhausting and destroying. You can use them both ways. If you prefer explosives that is your affair, not mine.

CUSINS. And it took a European war to stir mankind up to discover how to get harvests from the air !

LADY BRITOMART. Dont be wicked, Adolphus. You are encouraging Andrew. This is rather pretty, and no doubt very wonderful ; but it is immoral ; and I refuse to admire it. I have had enough of this. I am going home.

UNDERSHAFT. Not yet, my love. You must see where our men live. [*Leading the way out*] Come, Euripides : you think that nitrates are good for nothing but death. You shall see the sort of life they produce.

They go out, Lady Britomart coming last with Stephen.

LADY BRITOMART. Stephen : you have not uttered a single word since we arrived. Do you want your father to think you have nothing to say about those dreadful names across the hill ?

STEPHEN. I thought at first that they were in horribly bad taste. But somehow the place is very wonderful. Undershaft and Lazarus are very big people. I had rather say nothing until I have seen everything.

He goes out, his mother following, shaking her head ; for he is impressed and shaken, and shews it.

A grand square. The buildings are churches and temples in various styles of architecture. There is a Russian Greek Church brilliantly tinselled, a mosque, a Shinto temple, an Indian Jain temple, various Free Church meeting houses, two Church of England edifices, Protestant with spire and Anglican with tower, and a Roman Catholic church in Italian XII century taste with Virgin and crosses. And there is a round Labor Church, with the inscription "NO MAN IS GOOD ENOUGH TO BE ANOTHER MAN'S MASTER."

Undershaft and his party arrive.

CUSINS. What on earth is all this?

UNDERSHAFT. Its official name is The Meeting Place of All the Religions. But as that is too long a title for everyday use the men call it Piety Square.

LADY BRITOMART. You should not allow it, Andrew. You should learn how to keep your employees in order.

BARBARA. Is the real meeting place of all the religions a cannon foundry?

UNDERSHAFT. Yes: they are all agreed on that. You are yourself a major in a fighting army.

BARBARA. I am nothing now. When I fought it was to fight the devil, not to kill.

UNDERSHAFT. Fighting that is not to kill is not fighting at all. And they all call their adversaries the devil. There is a Salvation barracks here for you, if you wish, dear. And you, Euripides, shall have a temple of Dionysos. Or perhaps a little private oratory at the back of your office.

CUSINS. My office! What do you mean?

UNDERSHAFT. Pardon: I forgot that we have not come to that yet. The remark was prophetic. Shall we have a closer look at the buildings?

SARAH. Whats the Indian one? May we go in?

UNDERSHAFT. It is a Jain temple: a reproduction of the most famous one in the world. You may not worship there without washing yourself all over; but you can see everything quite well without overstepping the thresholds of the shrines.

SARAH. Let us go in. I think I should like to be a Jain.

LOMAX [*sings*] My Jane, my Jane, my pretty Jane, why dost thou look so shy?

LADY BRITOMART. Will nothing make you behave yourself, Charles? Remember that this is a sacred place, though the misguided worshippers are heathen idolators.

They go into the temple, and stop before one of the shrines, in which is a seated image. It fascinates them.

BARBARA. How utterly wonderful! Perfect peace! Perfect beauty! I think I shall become a Jain too. What god is it?

UNDERSHAFT. It is not a god. It is supposed to be only a wiseacre of some sort; but it is really a symbol. I am afraid it is worshipped and prayed to as a god, though the Jains hold that God is something beyond us with which they dare not meddle.

LOMAX [*even he is impressed*] It's quite awfully peaceful. Bad for the cannon trade, though, isnt it?

UNDERSHAFT. Not at all. We made these figures here.

CUSINS. You made those marvellous figures! I refuse to believe it.

UNDERSHAFT. One of our troubles here used to be the waste of good gunmetal involved in making cannons. This went on until I had to visit India on business. I was greatly struck by these figures, especially as they were quite new; for I had enough waste metal here to supply all India with them. I found they were made in a certain place by a certain set of native workmen, and nowhere else. I went to that place and bought up the whole concern, workmen and all. The wages I offered were of course far beyond anything they had ever dreamt of. I promised them a temple as well: you are now in it. Sometimes, when my nerves are overwrought I come in here and sit for an hour before this shrine while a priest recites prayers in a language of which I do not understand one word. It soothes me as nothing else does. This Jain religion is far ahead of anything we have in the west.

STEPHEN. You mean, I presume, except the Church of England.

UNDERSHAFT. We have two: a Protestant Low Church and an Anglican Ritualist. But somehow I never go into them.

LADY BRITOMART. Andrew: you grow wickeder and wickeder. Children: come away at once. There is some uncanny magic about this place: that figure will convert us all to Indian idolatry if we stay here any longer. Come.

She leads the way out. They follow reluctantly.

Exterior of the Shinto temple. The party as before.

UNDERSHAFT. This is where our Japanese experts worship.

LOMAX. The Shinto shop?

UNDERSHAFT. We call it a temple. There is nothing special inside except a priest who will expect you to give him a penny for a stick of incense to burn at the altar.

LADY BRITOMART. I shall most certainly do nothing of the sort. I will not go in.

UNDERSHAFT. You need not. But the temple is politically important to us here.

STEPHEN. How, pray?

UNDERSHAFT. Well, as Mr Lomax said, it is the temple of the Totalitarian State.

CUSINS. Do not forget that I am a collector of religions, Machiavelli. I happen to know all about Shinto. I know, for instance, that the Shinto Totalitarian State is personified by the divine emperor, descended from the sun, who owns everything.

UNDERSHAFT. Precisely.

CUSINS. Then does the Japanese Mikado own everything here?

UNDERSHAFT. No. I own everything here. As a foundling I may be descended from the sun. At all events I am the divine emperor.

LADY BRITOMART. Oh, this is beyond bearing. Andrew: I cannot breathe here. I must get back to some part of England where you dont own everything, and where everyone knows that you are a vulgar tradesman and not a divine emperor. Children: come away at once.

STEPHEN. I think not, mother. I will see this thing through.

CUSINS. I confess to being enormously amused. The discovery of Machiavelli as a divine emperor was worth living for.

LOMAX. Well, I can't help feeling that there is a certain amount of tosh about this last Shinto touch. I am not saying anything against it, you know.

LADY BRITOMART. You may think it a joke; but it is no joke to me. I am a Liberal; and without an atmosphere of freedom I suffocate.

BARBARA. It is easy to be a Liberal in Wilton Crescent on a divine emperor's millions. Not so easy at the East End, where women earn tuppence hapenny an hour, and families pay four shillings a week for an attic or a damp cellar to live in. I have seen enough of the toy temples where Indians worship you. Shew me where our own people live, and where they worship God.

UNDERSHAFT. I have reserved that for the last, my dear. We shall finish up with the places where the workers own everything, and I own nothing. You shall see how they live in their own houses, buy at their own shops, eat at their own restaurants, amuse themselves in their own theatres, and send their children to their own schools. It makes it very difficult for them to leave my employment. But then they do not want to leave it.

LADY BRITOMART. Slavery, I call it.

UNDERSHAFT. You would, my dear. But there is plenty of your pet political freedom here. Let me shew you.

They pass on to the Labor Church.

LADY BRITOMART. What is written up there round the top?

CUSINS. "No man is good enough to be another man's master." A famous maxim of William Morris, a great poet, a great communist, a great craftsman, and a great manufacturer. I still buy his curtains and wall-papers. I cannot afford his printed books. They cost hundreds.

LADY BRITOMART. Then he was also a very great hypocrite. Not good enough to be another man's master! He was everyman's master. I remember him quite well. He wore a blue shirt and no tie.

They go in.

The Labor Church, pillared and roofed like a church, has a platform instead of an altar, and a vast organ over it. Busts in all directions of the heroes and heroines of Labor.

UNDERSHAFT. Here are all the great revolutionists and socialists for you. That is Morris himself in the middle before the platform: Saint William of Kelmscott they call him. And all the rest: Robert Owen, Marx and Engels and Ferdinand Lassalle, Wells and Shaw and the Webbs; Hyndman and Cunninghame Graham and Kropotkin; Tolstoy and some new Russians called Bolsheviks: all of them the reddest of Reds. Revolutionary agitators draw the largest audiences here : they are usually the best speakers. I seldom speak in public ; but when I do I speak here.

STEPHEN. But do you allow seditious speeches to be made here ?

UNDERSHAFT. Of course : that is what the place is for. It is the Undershaft safety valve. Our people can talk here ; and as long as men can talk politics they will never do anything else except work for their daily bread.

BARBARA. May I hold a prayer meeting here ?

UNDERSHAFT. If you like. But there are Salvation barracks available. You will get a better attendance in them.

LOMAX. This place must cost a lot of money. Have you to pay for it ?

UNDERSHAFT. It pays for itself. There is a charge for admission at our concerts.

SARAH. Have you an orchestra .

UNDERSHAFT. We have the best orchestra in the world, and the best conductors, and the best singers. We pay them handsomely for one performance, which we televise and record so that we can reproduce it as often as we like.

LOMAX. I say : could you give us a spot of it now ?

UNDERSHAFT. Yes : I have had my favorite record put in ready for you. The announcer will explain. Let us sit in this row : it is the best for hearing.

They do so.

UNDERSHAFT. You will find a switch at the back of the seat in front of you. Push it over to the right.

LADY BRITOMART [*fingering it*] This one ?

UNDERSHAFT. Yes. Dont be afraid : it wont hurt you.

Lady Britomart pushes the switch over. Instantly the empty platform becomes an orchestra of a hundred performers in evening dress tuning their instruments. Behind them is the chorus, a small body of good singers, not a mob of amateurs. In front are seated four principal singers. The conductor's desk is vacant. The announcer comes on, and with a gesture signals to the band for silence. The tuning stops.

ANNOUNCER. What you are about to hear is a fragment from a dead opera by the Italian composer Giacomo Rossini, who in Europe a hundred years ago ranked as high as Handel in our own country. The subject is the miraculous passage through the Red Sea by the Israelites in their flight from Egypt.

But nowadays this has no appeal to our own destiny and our own troubles, consequently no importance for us. To make it live again we have interpreted the Red Sea as a symbol of the Socialist revolution on which our most glorious hopes and our deadliest fears are fixed. In the same agonizing throes of faith, hope, and terror must Moses have confronted the waves of the mighty sea that raged between his people and the promised land. We have not altered a note of the music: we have only given it such a wealth of orchestration as Rossini would himself have given it had the great resources of Undershaft and Lazarus been within his reach. The words alone are brought up to date. For Rossini at his greatest today there is only one conductor: Arturo Toscanini.

Toscanini enters, baton in hand, and takes his place at the conductor's desk.

ANNOUNCER. Ladies and gentlemen: Arturo Toscanini. [*He leaves the platform*].

Toscanini raises his baton; and the quartet and chorus from Rossini's Moses in Egypt follows, accompanied by the Wagnerian orchestra. At the famous modulation into G major the organ is added. The words are as follows.

RECITATIVE AND CHORUS

BASS SOLO. In this our hour of darkness
We warsmiths of the cannons
Where do we stand today?

CHORUS. We forge our own destruction
We shall be slain who slay.

BASS SOLO. Then from the gods who fail us
Ourselves must win the sway.

MAJOR BARBARA

I

QUARTET AND CHORUS

BASS SOLO. O thou great soul of all .
Say where but here within us
The answer to our call
Shall we, thy servants, find ?

CHORUS. Say where but here within us
Shall we the answer find ?

SOLO QUARTET. Say where ?

CHORUS. In ourselves.

II

TENOR SOLO. Shall we not then arise
And in our hearts the power
We sought for in the skies
Find ready to our hands ?

CHORUS. In heart and brain discover
The godhead in our hands

SOLO QUARTET. Where else ?

CHORUS. In our hands.

III

SOPRANO SOLO. From Women's tortured hearts
Their slaughtered sons lamenting
I cry against these arts
That slay what we create.

CHORUS. Creation, not destruction,
Shall henceforth make us great.

SOLO QUARTET. Dare we hope ?

CHORUS. Yes : we dare.

IV

Soloists and Chorus with Organ ad lib.

ALL. To thee the god within us
We trust the world to win us.
Creation, not destruction,
Henceforth shall make us great.

SOPRANO SOLO. Us great.

CHORUS. Henceforth.

The players and singers vanish, leaving the platform empty as before.

UNDERSHAFT. Well? what did you think of it?

LADY BRITOMART. I loathed it. My mother used to play Thalberg's variations on that air; and she tried to force me to learn them too. I have hated music ever since.

LOMAX. I could hear that it was classical music. It made a devil of a noise.

UNDERSHAFT [*rising*] Come! it is time for lunch: you must all be hungry.

They all rise eagerly and make for the door.

LADY BRITOMART. I hope we can depend on your cookery, Andrew.

UNDERSHAFT. You shall have what my workers eat.

LADY BRITOMART [*stopping*] Is there nothing better here, Andrew?

UNDERSHAFT. There is nothing better anywhere. Do not be afraid. Come!

A park surrounding a colossal modern forty storey mansion. The party arrives at the entrance in its cars, and alights there.

LOMAX. Is this part of the show?

UNDERSHAFT. It is part of the show. It is where our younger workers prefer to live. The young wives insist on service flats, though we have plenty of bungalows for them.

BARBARA. Service flats! Do you mean that the young women dont know how to cook and wash and do their own housework?

UNDERSHAFT. Not at all. They have been most thoroughly and carefully taught how to do every kind of domestic work. The result is that nothing will induce them to do it. They know too much about it. They prefer to earn wages in the workshops and be waited on by professional servants when they go home.

LADY BRITOMART. I'll stop my subscription to the Domestic

Training Institution at once. I never heard of such a thing.

They go in. In the entrance hall there are several automatic lifts : one marked EXPRESS. Undershaft presses the button of the Express lift, which comes down.

UNDERSHAFT. Youll lunch on the thirty-second floor [*he opens the grill of the lift, and ushers them in*].

The lift ascends. When they leave it, Undershaft conducts them to a handsome salon with big windows. A table is ready for lunch with a luxurious display of linen and silver and flowers.

LADY BRITOMART [*surveying the table critically*] The table is laid for five only. We are six.

UNDERSHAFT. You forget, my love, that I dont lunch. It is a modern habit I have never been able to acquire. A penny roll and a glass of milk in my office is enough for me. I must leave you now for an hour or so to see after my office business. It will be a relief for you to get rid of me for a while.

ALL EXCEPT BARBARA AND LADY BRITOMART [*politely murmuring*] Oh no. Not at all.

BARBARA [*explosively*] Yes it will. We cant talk about all these upsetting things in front of you. I want an hour's respite and some food.

UNDERSHAFT. You shall have both, my love. But first let me shew you where my older workpeople live. You can see it all from this window.

They crowd to the window he indicates.

The view from the window is of a green valley dotted with bungalows of various design : each with its verandah and garden.

LOMAX. Garden city notion, what ?

UNDERSHAFT. They call it a garden suburb. I'm sorry to say they are all incorrigible snobs. You must be careful what you say when they are listening. Now if youll come to this window youll see where to find me in my own office.

They move expectantly to the opposite window. It commands a view of an ancient slag heap, now an apparently natural hill dotted with separate wooden sheds, and surmounted by a parapet and firestep on which is mounted an obsolete black cannon, short in the barrel and thick in the breech, without ornament of any kind.

UNDERSHAFT. That is where we handle high explosives. Any of those sheds may blow up at any moment. An explosion costs nothing but a shed and perhaps a casualty or two. The hill is called Thundercrest: it is the oldest part of the concern; and the Undershafts still like to do a good deal of their business there in the old shed that was meant for the clerk of the works. I leave the official bureau with its filing cabinets and board room and luxurious furniture and carpets and so on to Lazarus, who thoroughly enjoys them. I am more at home in the shed.

SARAH. Whats the big black thing peeping over the wall at the top?

UNDERSHAFT. That old thing is the gun that made me famous. It was called the Woolwich Infant; but it was designed by me and made by me. It is a sort of keepsake: one of the few things I am really sentimental about. That is where youll find me when you have finished here. The chauffeur will drive you over. Remember the name: Thundercrest. [*He goes out*].

CUSINS. I am rather impressed by the possibility of any of those sheds blowing up at any moment. It has a horrible fascination for me; but I think I shall take Barbara home first.

LADY BRITOMART. You had better all go home. But I shall stay. I had rather be blown to bits than let Andrew think he has frightened me.

SARAH. Your sentiments are mine, respected parent.

BARBARA [*very emphatically*] AND mine.

Lunch is brought in.

BARBARA. At last. Grub.

All except Lady Britomart rush hungrily to seat themselves at table, anyhow.

LADY BRITOMART. Dont rush, children. Really, you are picking up your father's manners already. [*She takes the head of the table with dignity*].

They all eat greedily, exhausted by the wonders of Undershaft and Lazarus.

Thundercrest. A gun emplacement along the ridge of the hill, with the old fat black cannon (the Woolwich Infant) in the middle, aiming southward over a firestep which fortifies the whole length of the emplacement and is evidently much older than the cannon. On the grey masonry of its breastwork are slate panels with incised inscriptions, illegible except at close quarters. In utmost contrast to the ultra-modernity and fresh paint of the model factory town hidden on the far side of the hill, Thundercrest is centuries old. It is used only as a dumping place for junk. Old ammunition boxes, handy for visitors to sit on, abound. The quaintest objects are lifesize dummy soldiers in early Victorian uniforms, lying about anyhow and anywhere in their red coats, cockaded peaked headgear, epaulets, and belts on which the pipe-clay has long lost its lustre. Many of them have suffered gaping grapeshot wounds from which their straw entrails protrude grotesquely. One of them, fearfully gashed across the abdomen, has fallen in front of a very unimposing old brick edifice at the west end of the emplacement, with the word MANAGER over the door in the ugliest pre-Morrisian lettering. At the opposite end is one of the shabby old huts with which the hill is dotted. It is raised on posts and entered by a flight of wooden steps. The door is labelled DANGER in red ! ! *Near the cannon is a new-looking modern shell with a red band painted on it.*

The visiting party arrives, looking with some wonder at the prevailing disorder and decay.

Undershaft comes from the office, with a sheaf of telegrams in his hand.

UNDERSHAFT. Well, have you seen everything? I'm sorry I was called away. [*Indicating the telegrams*] Good news from the front.

STEPHEN. Another victory?

UNDERSHAFT. Oh, I dont know. Which side wins does not concern us here. No: the good news is that the aerial battleship is a tremendous success. At the first trial it has wiped out a fort with three hundred soldiers in it [*he pockets the telegrams*].

CUSINS [*from the platform*] Dummy soldiers?

UNDERSHAFT [*striding across to Stephen and kicking the disemboweled dummy out of his way*] No: the real thing.

Cusins and Barbara exchange glances. Then Cusins sits on the step and buries his face in his hands. Barbara gravely lays her hand on his shoulder. He looks up at her in whimsical desperation.

UNDERSHAFT. Well, Stephen, what do you think of the place?

STEPHEN. Oh, magnificent. A perfect triumph of modern industry. Frankly, my dear father, I have been a fool: I had no idea of what it all meant: of the wonderful forethought, the power of organization, the administrative capacity, the financial genius, the colossal capital it represents. I have been repeating to myself as I came through your streets "Peace hath her victories no less renowned than War." I have only one misgiving about it all.

UNDERSHAFT. Out with it.

STEPHEN. Well, I cannot help thinking that all this provision for every want of your workmen may sap their independence and weaken their sense of responsibility. Are you sure so much pampering is really good for the men's characters?

UNDERSHAFT. Well you see, my dear boy, when you are organizing civilization you have to make up your mind whether trouble and anxiety are good things or not. If you decide that they are, then, I take it, you simply dont organize civilization; and there you are, with trouble and anxiety enough to make us all angels! But if you decide the other way, you may as well go through with it. However, Stephen, our characters are safe here. A sufficient dose of anxiety is always provided by the fact that we may be blown to smithereens at any moment.

At the same moment the door of the shed is thrown abruptly open; and a foreman in overalls and list slippers comes out on the little landing and holds the door for Lomax, who appears in the doorway.

LOMAX [*with studied coolness*] My good fellow: you neednt get into a state of nerves. Nothing's going to happen to you; and I suppose it wouldnt be the end of the world if anything did. A little bit of British pluck is what you want, old chap. [*He descends and strolls across to Sarah*].

UNDERSHAFT [*to the foreman*] Anything wrong, Bilton?

BILTON [*with ironic calm*] Gentleman walked into the high explosives shed and lit a cigaret, sir: thats all.

UNDERSHAFT. Ah, quite so. [*Going over to Lomax*] Do you happen to remember what you did with the match?

LOMAX. Oh come! I'm not a fool. I took jolly good care to blow it out before I chucked it away.

BILTON. The top of it was red hot inside, sir.

LOMAX. Well, suppose it was! I didn't chuck it into any of your messes.

UNDERSHAFT. Think no more of it, Mr Lomax. By the way, would you mind lending me your matches.

LOMAX [*offering his box*] Certainly.

UNDERSHAFT. Thanks. [*He pockets the matches*].

LOMAX [*lecturing to the company generally*] You know, these high explosives dont go off like gunpowder, except when theyre in a gun. When theyre spread loose, you can put a match to them without the least risk: they just burn quietly like a bit of paper. [*Warming to the scientific interest of the subject*] Did you know that, Mr Undershaft? Have you ever tried?

UNDERSHAFT. Not on a large scale, Mr Lomax. Bilton will give you a sample of gun cotton when you are leaving if you ask him. You can experiment with it at home. [*Bilton looks puzzled*].

SARAH. Bilton will do nothing of the sort, papa. I suppose it's your business to blow up our enemies; but you might at least stop short of blowing up poor Cholly. [*Bilton gives it up and retires into the shed*].

LOMAX. My ownest, there is no danger. [*He sits beside her on the shell*].

LADY BRITOMART. Andrew: you shouldnt have let me see this place. To think of it being yours! and that you have kept it to yourself all these years!

UNDERSHAFT. It does not belong to me. I belong to it. It is the Undershaft inheritance.

LADY BRITOMART. It is not. Your cannons and chemicals may be the Undershaft inheritance; but the estate belongs to us. I wont give it up. I dont ask it any longer for Stephen—

STEPHEN [*interrupting her sharply*] I have not asked for it myself. The place is wonderful; but there is a Stevenage tradition as well as an Undershaft one. My future is in the Cabinet or Foreign Office, not in the counting house.

LADY BRITOMART. And leave Barbara to starve! Why should not Adolphus succeed to the inheritance? I could manage the town for him; and he can look after the cannons, if they are really necessary.

UNDERSHAFT. I should ask nothing better if Adolphus were a foundling. He is exactly the sort of new blood that is wanted in English business. Unfortunately he's not a foundling. [*He makes for the office door*].

CUSINS. How do you know? [*They all turn and stare at him*]. I think—Mind! I am not committing myself in any way as to my future course—but I think the foundling difficulty can be got over.

UNDERSHAFT. What do you mean?

CUSINS. Well, I have something to say which is in the nature of a confession.

SARAH.
LADY BRITOMART.
BARBARA.
STEPHEN. } Confession!

LOMAX. Oh I say!

CUSINS. Yes, a confession. Listen, all. Until I met Barbara I thought myself in the main an honorable, truthful man, because I wanted the approval of my conscience more than I wanted anything else. But the moment I saw Barbara, I wanted her far more than the approval of my conscience.

LADY BRITOMART. Adolphus !

CUSINS. It is true. You accused me yourself, Lady Brit, of joining the Army to worship Barbara ; and so I did. She bought my soul like a flower at a street corner ; but she bought it for herself.

UNDERSHAFT. What ! Not for Dionysos or another ?

CUSINS. Dionysos and all the others are in herself. I adored what was divine in her, and was therefore a true worshipper. But I was romantic about her too. I thought she was a woman of the people, and that a marriage with a professor of Greek would be far beyond the wildest social ambitions of her rank.

LADY BRITOMART. Adolphus ! !

LOMAX. Oh I say ! ! !

CUSINS. When I learnt the horrible truth—

LADY BRITOMART. What do you mean by the horrible truth, pray ?

CUSINS. That she was enormously rich ; that her grandfather was an earl ; that her father was the Prince of Darkness—

UNDERSHAFT. Chut !

CUSINS. —and that I was only an adventurer trying to catch a rich wife, then I stooped to deceive her about my birth.

BARBARA [*rising*] Dolly !

LADY BRITOMART. Your birth ! Now Adolphus, dont dare to make up a wicked story for the sake of these wretched cannons. Remember : I have seen photographs of your parents ; and the Agent General for South Western Australia knows them personally and has assured me that they are most respectable married people.

CUSINS. Their marriage was legal in Australia, but not in England. My mother is my father's deceased wife's sister ; and in this island I was consequently a foundling. [*Sensation*].

STEPHEN. But such marriages have been made legal in England.

CUSINS. Not until I was grown up. I was born and bred a bastard. That is all the tradition requires. What do you say, Machiavelli?

UNDERSHAFT. You are an educated man. That is against the tradition.

CUSINS. Once in ten thousand times it happens that the schoolboy is a born master of what they try to teach him. Greek has not destroyed my mind: it has nourished it. Besides, I did not learn it at an English public school.

UNDERSHAFT. Hm! Well, I cannot afford to be too particular: you have cornered the foundling market. Let it pass. You are eligible, Euripides: you are eligible.

BARBARA. Dolly: yesterday morning, when Stephen told us all about the tradition, you became very silent; and you have been strange and excited ever since. Were you thinking of your birth then?

CUSINS. When the finger of Destiny suddenly points at a man in the middle of his breakfast, it makes him thoughtful.

UNDERSHAFT. Aha! You have had your eye on the business, my young friend, have you?

CUSINS. Take care! There is an abyss of moral horror between me and your accursed aerial battleships.

UNDERSHAFT. Never mind the abyss for the present. Let us settle the practical details and leave your final decision open. You know that you will have to change your name. Do you object to that?

CUSINS. Would any man named Adolphus—any man called Dolly!—object to be called something else?

UNDERSHAFT. Good. Now, as to money! I propose to treat you handsomely from the beginning. You shall start at a thousand a year.

CUSINS [*with sudden heat, his spectacles twinkling with mischief*] A thousand! You dare offer a miserable thousand to the son-in-law of a millionaire! No, by Heavens, Machiavelli! you shall not sweat me. You cannot do without me; and I can do without you. I must have two thousand five hundred a year for two years. At the end of that time if I am a failure, I go. But if I am a success, and stay on, you must give me the other five thousand.

UNDERSHAFT. What other five thousand?

CUSINS. To make the two years up to five thousand a year. The two thousand five hundred is only half pay in case I should turn out a failure. The third year I must have ten per cent on the profits.

UNDERSHAFT [*taken aback*] Ten per cent! Why, man, do you know what my profits are?

CUSINS. Enormous, I hope: otherwise I shall require twentyfive per cent.

UNDERSHAFT. But, Mr Cusins, this is a serious matter of business. You are not bringing any capital into the concern.

CUSINS. What! no capital! Is my mastery of Greek no capital? Is my access to the subtlest thought, the loftiest poetry yet attained by humanity, no capital? My character! my intellect! my life! my career! what Barbara calls my soul! are these no capital? Say another word; and I double my salary.

UNDERSHAFT. Be reasonable—

CUSINS [*peremptorily*] Mr Undershaft: you have my terms. Take them or leave them.

UNDERSHAFT [*recovering himself*] Very well. I note your terms; and I offer you half.

CUSINS [*disgusted*] Half!

UNDERSHAFT [*firmly*] Half.

CUSINS. You call yourself a gentleman; and you offer me half!!

UNDERSHAFT. I do not call myself a gentleman; but I offer you half.

CUSINS. This to your future partner! your successor! your son-in-law!

BARBARA. You are selling your own soul, Dolly, not mine. Leave me out of the bargain, please.

UNDERSHAFT. Come! I will go a step further for Barbara's

sake. I will give you three fifths; but that is my last word.

CUSINS. Done!

LOMAX. Done in the eye! Why, *I* get only eight hundred, you know.

CUSINS. By the way, Mac, I am a classical scholar, not a mathematical one. Is three fifths more than half or less?

UNDERSHAFT. More, of course.

CUSINS. I would have taken two hundred and fifty. How you can succeed in business when you are willing to pay all that money to a University don who is obviously not worth a junior clerk's wages!—well! What will Lazarus say?

UNDERSHAFT. Lazarus is a gentle romantic Jew who cares for nothing but string quartets and stalls at fashionable theatres. He will be blamed for your rapacity in money matters, poor fellow! as he has hitherto been blamed for mine. You are a shark of the first order, Euripides. So much the better for the firm!

BARBARA. Is the bargain closed, Dolly? Does your soul belong to him now?

CUSINS. No: the price is settled: that is all. The real tug of war is still to come. What about the moral question?

LADY BRITOMART. There is no moral question in the matter at all, Adolphus. You must simply sell cannons and weapons to people whose cause is right and just, and refuse them to foreigners and criminals.

UNDERSHAFT [*determinedly*] No: none of that. You must keep the true faith of an Armorer, or you dont come in here.

CUSINS. What on earth is the true faith of an Armorer?

UNDERSHAFT. To give arms to all men who offer an honest price for them, without respect of persons or principles: to Royalist and Republican, to Communist and Capitalist, to Protestant and Catholic, to burglar and policeman, to black man white man and yellow man, to all sorts and conditions, all nationalities, all faiths, all follies, all causes and all crimes. Have you read these letters cut into the wall behind you? They are the last words of the wisdom of the Undershafts since their beginnings on this spot. Here is the first: IF GOD GAVE THE HAND, LET NOT MAN WITHHOLD THE SWORD. The second: ALL HAVE THE RIGHT TO FIGHT: NONE HAVE THE RIGHT TO JUDGE. The third: TO MAN THE WEAPON: TO HEAVEN THE VICTORY. The fourth had no literary turn; so he wrote nothing; but he sold cannons to Napoleon under the nose of George the Third. The fifth: PEACE SHALL NOT PREVAIL SAVE WITH A SWORD IN HER HAND. The sixth, my master, was the best of all. NOTHING IS EVER DONE IN THIS WORLD UNTIL MEN ARE PREPARED TO KILL ONE ANOTHER IF IT IS NOT DONE. After that, there was nothing left for me to say. So I shall write up, simply, UNASHAMED.

CUSINS. My good Machiavelli, I shall certainly write something up on the wall; only, as I shall write it in Greek, you wont be able to read it. But as to your Armorer's faith, if I take my neck out of the noose of my own morality I am not going to put it into the noose of yours. I shall sell cannons to whom I please and refuse them to whom I please. So there!

UNDERSHAFT. From the moment when you become Andrew Undershaft, you will never do as you please again. Dont come here lusting for power, young man.

CUSINS. If power were my aim I should not come here for it. You have no power.

UNDERSHAFT. None of my own, certainly.

CUSINS. I have more power than you, more will. You do not drive this place: it drives you. And what drives the place?

UNDERSHAFT [*enigmatically*] A will of which I am a part.

BARBARA [*startled*] Father! Do you know what you are saying? or are you laying a snare for my soul?

CUSINS. Dont listen to his metaphysics, Barbara. The place is driven by Capitalist money hunters; and he is their slave.

UNDERSHAFT. Not necessarily. Remember the Armorers' Faith. I will take an order from a good man as cheerfully as from a bad one. If you good people prefer preaching and shirking to buying my weapons and fighting the money hunters, dont blame me. I can make cannons : I cannot make courage and conviction. Bah ! you tire me, Euripides, with your morality mongering. Ask Barbara : she understands. [*He takes Barbara's hands, looking powerfully into her eyes*] Tell him, my love, what power really means.

BARBARA. [*hypnotized*] Before I joined the Salvation Army, I was in my own power ; and the consequence was that I never knew what to do with myself. When I joined it, I had not time enough for all the things I had to do.

UNDERSHAFT [*approvingly*] Just so. And why was that, do you suppose ?

BARBARA. Yesterday I should have said, because I was in the power of God. [*She withdraws her hands from his with a power equal to his own*]. But you came and shewed me that I was in the power of Bodger and Undershaft. Today I feel—oh ! how can I put it into words ? Sarah : do you remember the earthquake at Cannes, when we were little children ?—how little the surprise of the first shock mattered compared to the dread and horror of waiting for the second ? That is how I feel in this place today. I stood on the rock I thought eternal ; and without a word of warning it reeled and crumbled under me. I was safe with an infinite wisdom watching me, an army marching to Salvation with me ; and in a moment, at a stroke of your pen in your cheque book, I stood alone ; and the heavens were empty. That was the first shock of the earthquake : I am waiting for the second.

UNDERSHAFT. Come, come, my daughter ! dont make too much of your little tinpot tragedy. What do we do here when we spend years of work and thought and thousands of pounds of solid cash on a new gun or an aerial battleship that turns out just a hairsbreadth wrong after all ? Scrap it. Scrap it without wasting another hour or another pound on it. Well, you have made for yourself something that you call a morality or a religion or what not. It doesnt fit the facts. Well, scrap it. Scrap it and get one that does fit. That is what is wrong with the world at present. It scraps its obsolete steam engines and dynamos ; but it wont scrap its old prejudices and its old moralities and its old religions and its old political constitutions. Whats the result? In machinery it does very well ; but in morals and religion and politics it is working at a loss that brings it nearer bankruptcy every year. Dont persist in that folly. If your old religion broke down yesterday, get a newer and a better one for tomorrow.

BARBARA. Oh how gladly I would take a better one to my soul ! But you offer me a worse one. [*Turning on him with sudden vehemence*]. Justify yourself : shew me some light through the darkness of this dreadful place, with its beautifully clean workshops, and respectable workmen, and model homes.

UNDERSHAFT. Cleanliness and respectability do not need justification, Barbara : they justify themselves. I see no darkness here, no dreadfulness. In your Salvation shelter I saw poverty, misery, cold and hunger. You gave them bread and treacle and dreams of heaven. I give from three pound ten a week to twelve thousand a year. They find their own dreams ; but I look after the drainage.

BARBARA. And their souls ?

UNDERSHAFT. I save their souls just as I saved yours.

BARBARA. You saved my soul ! What do you mean ?

UNDERSHAFT. I fed you and clothed you and housed you. I took care that you should have money enough to live handsomely—more than enough ; so that you could be wasteful, careless, generous. That saved your soul from the seven deadly sins.

BARBARA [*bewildered*] The seven deadly sins !

UNDERSHAFT. Yes, the deadly seven. [*Counting on his fingers*] Food, clothing, firing, rent, taxes, respectability and children. Nothing can lift those seven millstones from Man's neck but money ; and the spirit cannot soar until the millstones are lifted. I lifted them from your spirit. I enabled Barbara to become Major Barbara; and I saved her from the crime of poverty.

CUSINS. Do you call poverty a crime?

UNDERSHAFT. The worst of crimes. Poverty blights whole cities; spreads horrible pestilences; strikes dead the very souls of all who come within sight, sound, or smell of it. What *you* call crime is nothing: a murder here and a theft there, a blow now and a curse then: what do they matter? they are only the accidents and illnesses of life: there are not fifty genuine professional criminals in London. But there are millions of poor people, abject people, dirty people, sick people, ignorant people, ill fed, ill clothed people, poisoning us, forcing us to organize unnatural cruelties for fear they should rise against us and drag us down into their abyss. Only fools fear crime: we all fear poverty. Pah! [*turning to Barbara*] you talk of your half-saved ruffian in West Ham: you accuse me of dragging his soul back to perdition. Well, bring him to me here; and I will drag his soul back again to salvation for you. Not by words and dreams; but by three pound ten the five day week, a sound house in a healthy street, and a permanent job. In three weeks he will have a bowler hat and a chapel sitting: before the end of the year he will shake hands with a duchess at a Primrose League meeting, and join the Conservative Party.

BARBARA. And will he be the better for that?

UNDERSHAFT. You know he will. Dont be a hypocrite, Barbara. He will be better fed, better housed, better clothed, better behaved; and his children will be pounds heavier and bigger. That will be better than an American cloth mattress in a shelter, chopping firewood, eating bread and treacle, and being forced to kneel down from time to time to thank heaven for it: knee drill, I think you call it. It is cheap work converting starving men with a Bible in one hand and a slice of bread in the other. I will undertake to convert West Ham to Mahometanism on the same terms. Try your hand on my men: their souls are hungry because their bodies are full.

BARBARA. And leave the east end to starve?

UNDERSHAFT [*his energetic tone dropping into one of bitter and brooding remembrance*] *I* was an east ender. I moralized and starved until one day I swore that I would be a full-fed free man at all costs; that nothing should stop me except a bullet, neither reason nor morals nor the lives of other men. I said "Thou shalt starve ere I starve"; and with that word I became free and great. I was a dangerous man until I had my will: now I am a useful, beneficent, kindly person. That is the history of most self-made millionaires, I fancy. When it is the history of every Englishman we shall have an England worth living in.

LADY BRITOMART. Stop making speeches, Andrew. This is not the place for them.

UNDERSHAFT [*punctured*] My dear: I have no other means of conveying my ideas.

LADY BRITOMART. Your ideas are nonsense. You got on because you were selfish and unscrupulous.

UNDERSHAFT. Not at all. I had the strongest scruples about poverty and starvation. Your moralists are quite unscrupulous about both: they make virtues of them. I had rather be a thief than a pauper. I had rather be a murderer than a slave. I dont want to be either; but if you force the alternative on me, then, by Heaven, I'll choose the braver and more moral one. I hate poverty and slavery worse than any other crimes whatsoever. And let me tell you this. Poverty and slavery have stood up for centuries to your sermons and speeches and leading articles: they will not stand up to my machine guns. Dont preach at them: dont reason with them. Kill them.

BARBARA. Killing. Is that your remedy for everything?

UNDERSHAFT. It is the final test of conviction, the only lever strong enough to overturn a social system, the only way of saying Must. Let six hundred and seventy fools loose in the streets; and three policemen can scatter them. But huddle them together in a chamber in Westminster; and let them go through certain ceremonies and call themselves certain names until at last they get the courage to kill; and your six hundred and seventy fools become a government. Your pious mob fills up ballot papers and imagines it is governing its masters; but the ballot paper that really governs is the paper that has a bullet wrapped up in it.

CUSINS. That is perhaps why, like most intelligent people, I never vote.

UNDERSHAFT. Vote! Bah! When you vote, you only change the names of the Cabinet. When you shoot, you pull down governments, inaugurate new epochs, abolish old orders and set up new. Is that historically true, Mr Learned Man, or is it not?

CUSINS. It is historically true. I loathe having to admit it. I repudiate your sentiments. I abhor your nature. I defy you in every possible way. Still, it is true. But it ought not to be true.

UNDERSHAFT. Ought! ought! ought! ought! ought! Are you going to spend your life saying ought, like the rest of our moralists? Turn your oughts into shalls, man. Come and make explosives with me. Whatever can blow men up can blow society up. The history of the world is the history of those who had courage enough to embrace this truth. Have you the courage to embrace it, Barbara?

LADY BRITOMART. Barbara: I positively forbid you to listen to your father's abominable wickedness. And you, Adolphus, ought to know better than to go about saying that wrong things are true. What does it matter whether they are true if they are wrong?

UNDERSHAFT. What does it matter whether they are wrong if they are true?

LADY BRITOMART. Children: come home instantly. Andrew: I am exceedingly sorry I allowed you to call on us. You are wickeder than ever. Come at once.

BARBARA [*shaking her head*] It's no use running away from wicked people, mamma.

LADY BRITOMART. It is every use. It shews your disapprobation of them.

BARBARA. It does not save them.

LADY BRITOMART. I see that you are going to disobey me. Sarah: are you coming home or are you not?

SARAH. I daresay it's very wicked of papa to make cannons; but I dont think I shall cut him on that account.

LOMAX [*pouring oil on the troubled waters*] The fact is, you know, there is a certain amount of tosh about this notion of wickedness. It doesnt work. You must look at facts. Not that I would say a word in favor of anything wrong; but then, you see, all sorts of chaps are always doing all sorts of things; and we have to fit them in somehow, dont you know. What I mean is that you cant go cutting everybody; and thats about what it comes to. [*Their rapt attention to his eloquence makes him nervous*]. Perhaps I dont make myself clear.

LADY BRITOMART. You are lucidity itself, Charles. Because Andrew is successful and has plenty of money to give to Sarah, you will flatter him and encourage him in his wickedness.

LOMAX [*unruffled*] Well, where the carcase is, there will the eagles be gathered, dont you know. [*To Undershaft*] Eh? What?

UNDERSHAFT. Precisely. By the way, may I call you Charles?

LOMAX. Delighted. Cholly is the usual ticket.

UNDERSHAFT [*to Lady Britomart*] Biddy—

LADY BRITOMART [*violently*] Dont dare call me Biddy. Charles Lomax: you are a fool. Adolphus Cusins: you are a Jesuit. Stephen: you are a prig. Sarah: you are a nonentity. Barbara: you are a lunatic. Andrew: you are a vulgar tradesman. Now you all know my opinion; and my conscience is clear, at all events [*she sits down on an ammunition box with a vehemence that almost splits it*].

UNDERSHAFT. My dear: you are the incarnation of morality. [*She snorts*]. Your conscience is clear and your duty done when you have called everybody names.

Come, Euripides! it is getting late; and we all want to go home. Make up your mind.

CUSINS. Understand this, you old demon. You have me in a horrible dilemma. I want Barbara.

UNDERSHAFT. Like all young men, you greatly exaggerate the difference between one young woman and another.

BARBARA. Quite true, Dolly.

CUSINS. I also want to avoid being a rascal.

UNDERSHAFT [*with biting contempt*] You lust for personal righteousness, for self-approval, for what you call a good conscience, for what Barbara calls salvation, for what I call patronizing people who are not so lucky as yourself.

CUSINS. I do not: all the poet in me recoils from being a good man. But there are things in me that I must reckon with. Pity—

UNDERSHAFT. Pity! The scavenger of misery.

CUSINS. Well, love.

UNDERSHAFT. I know. You love the needy and the outcast: you love the oppressed races, the negro, the Indian ryot, the underdog everywhere. Do you love the Japanese? Do you love the French? Do you love the English?

CUSINS. No. Every true Englishman detests the English. We are the wickedest nation on earth; and our success is a moral horror.

UNDERSHAFT. That is what comes of your gospel of love, is it?

CUSINS. May I not love even my father-in-law?

UNDERSHAFT. Who wants your love, man? By what right do you take the liberty of offering it to me? I will have your due heed and respect, or I will kill you. But your love! Damn your impertinence!

CUSINS [*grinning*] I may not be able to control my affections, Mac.

UNDERSHAFT. You are fencing, Euripides. You are weakening: your grip is slipping. Come! try your last weapon. Pity and love have broken in your hand: forgiveness is still left.

CUSINS. No: forgiveness is a beggar's refuge. I am with you there: we must pay our debts.

UNDERSHAFT. Well said. Come! you will suit me. Remember the words of Plato.

CUSINS. Plato! *You* dare quote Plato to *me*!

UNDERSHAFT. Plato says, my friend, that society cannot be saved until either the Professors of Greek take to making gunpowder, or else the makers of gunpowder become Professors of Greek.

CUSINS. Oh, tempter! cunning tempter!

UNDERSHAFT. Come! choose, man, choose.

CUSINS. But perhaps Barbara will not marry me if I make the wrong choice.

BARBARA. Perhaps not.

CUSINS [*desperately perplexed*] You hear!

BARBARA. Father: do you love nobody?

UNDERSHAFT. I love my best friend.

LADY BRITOMART. And who is that, pray?

UNDERSHAFT. My bravest enemy. That is the man who keeps me up to the mark.

CUSINS. You know, the creature is really a sort of poet in his way. Suppose he is a great man, after all!

UNDERSHAFT. Suppose you stop talking and make up your mind, my young friend.

CUSINS. But you are driving me against my nature. I hate war.

UNDERSHAFT. Hatred is the coward's revenge for being intimidated. Dare you make war on war? Here are the means: Mr Lomax is sitting on them.

LOMAX [*springing up*] Oh I say! You dont mean that this thing is loaded, do you? My ownest: come off it.

SARAH [*sitting placidly on the shell*] If I am to be blown up, the more thoroughly it is done the better. Dont fuss, Cholly.

LOMAX [*to Undershaft, strongly remonstrant*] Your own daughter, you know!

UNDERSHAFT. So I see. [*To Cusins*] Well, my friend, may we expect you here at six tomorrow morning?

CUSINS [*firmly*] Not on any account. I will see the whole

establishment blown up with its own dynamite before I will get up at five. My hours are healthy, rational hours : eleven to five.

UNDERSHAFT. Come when you please : before a week you will come at six and stay until I turn you out for the sake of your health. [*Calling*] Bilton ! [*He turns to Lady Britomart, who rises*]. My dear : let us leave these two young people to themselves for a moment. [*Bilton appears at the door of the shed*]. I am going to take you through the cordite shed.

BILTON [*barring the way*] You cant take anything explosive in here, sir.

LADY BRITOMART. What do you mean ? Are you alluding to me ?

BILTON [*unmoved*] No, maam. Mr Undershaft has the other gentleman's matches in his pocket.

LADY BRITOMART [*abruptly*] Oh ! I beg your pardon. [*She goes into the shed*].

UNDERSHAFT. Quite right, Bilton, quite right : here you are. [*He gives Bilton the box of matches*]. Come, Stephen. Come, Charles, Bring Sarah. [*He passes into the shed*].

Bilton opens the box and deliberately drops the matches into the fire-bucket.

LOMAX. Oh ! I say [*Bilton stolidly hands him the empty box*]. Infernal nonsense ! Pure scientific ignorance ! [*He goes in*].

SARAH. Am I all right, Bilton ?

BILTON. Youll have to put on list slippers, miss : thats all. Weve got em inside. [*She goes in*].

STEPHEN [*very seriously to Cusins*] Dolly, old fellow, think. Think before you decide. Do you feel that you are a sufficiently practical man ? It is a huge undertaking : an enormous responsibility. All this mass of business will be Greek to you.

CUSINS. Oh, I think it will be much less difficult than Greek.

STEPHEN. Well, I just want to say this before I leave you to yourselves. Dont let anything I have said about right and wrong prejudice you against this great chance in life. I have satisfied myself that the business is one of the highest character. [*Emotionally*] I am very proud of my father. I— [*Unable to proceed, he presses Cusins' hand and goes hastily into the shed, followed by Bilton*].

Barbara and Cusins, left alone together, look at one another silently.

CUSINS. Barbara : I am going to accept this offer.

BARBARA. I thought you would.

CUSINS. You understand, dont you, that I had to decide without consulting you. If I had thrown the burden of the choice on you, you would sooner or later have despised me for it.

BARBARA. Yes : I did not want you to sell your soul for me any more than for this inheritance.

CUSINS. It is not the sale of my soul that troubles me : I have sold it too often to care about that. I have sold it for a professorship. I have sold it for an income. I have sold it to escape being imprisoned for refusing to pay taxes for hangmen's ropes and unjust wars and things that I abhor. What is all human conduct but the daily and hourly sale of our souls ? What I am now selling it for is neither money nor position nor comfort, but for reality and power.

BARBARA. You know that you will have no power, and that he has none.

CUSINS. I know. It is not for myself alone. I want to make power for the world.

BARBARA. I want to make power for the world too ; but it must be spiritual power.

CUSINS. I think all power is spiritual : these cannons will not go off by themselves. I have tried to make spiritual power by teaching Greek. But the world can never be really touched by a dead language and a dead civilization. The people must have power ; and the people cannot have Greek. Now the power that is made here can be wielded by all men.

BARBARA. Power to burn women's houses down and kill their sons and tear their husbands to pieces.

CUSINS. You cannot have power for good without having

power for evil too. Even mother's milk nourishes murderers as well as heroes. This power which only tears men's bodies to pieces has never been so horribly abused as the intellectual power, the imaginative power, the poetic, religious power that can enslave men's souls. As a teacher of Greek I gave the rich man an intellectual weapon against the poor man. I now want to give the poor man material weapons against the intellectual man. I want to arm him against the lawyers, the doctors, the priests, the literary men, the professors, the artists, and the politicians, who, once in authority, are more disastrous and tyrannical than all the fools, rascals, and impostors. I want a power simple enough for common men to use, yet strong enough to force the intellectual oligarchy to use its genius for the general good.

BARBARA. Is there no higher power than that [*pointing to the shell*] ?

CUSINS. Yes ; but that power can destroy the higher powers just as a tiger can destroy a man : therefore Man must master that power first. I admitted this when the Turks and Greeks were last at war. My best pupil went out to fight for Hellas. My parting gift to him was not a copy of Plato's Republic, but a revolver and a hundred Undershaft cartridges. The blood of every Turk he shot—if he shot any—is on my head as well as on Undershaft's. That act committed me to this place for ever. Your father's challenge has beaten me. Dare I make war on war ? I dare. I must. I will. And now, is it all over between us ?

BARBARA [*touched by his evident dread of her answer*] Silly baby Dolly ! How could it be !

CUSINS [*overjoyed*] Then you—you—you— Oh for my drum ! [*He flourishes imaginary drumsticks*].

BARBARA [*angered by his levity*] Take care, Dolly, take care. Oh, if only I could get away from you and from father and from it all ! if I could have the wings of a dove and fly away to heaven !

CUSINS. And leave me !

BARBARA. Yes, you, and all the other naughty mischievous children of men. But I cant. I was happy in the Salvation Army for a moment. I escaped from the world into a paradise of enthusiasm and prayer and soul saving; but the moment our money ran short, it all came back to Bodger: it was he who saved our people: he, and the Prince of Darkness, my papa. Undershaft and Bodger: their hands stretch everywhere: when we feed a starving fellow creature, it is with their bread, because there is no other bread; when we tend the sick, it is in the hospitals they endow; if we turn from the churches they build, we must kneel on the stones of the streets they pave. As long as that lasts, there is no getting away from them. Turning our backs on Bodger and Undershaft is turning our backs on life.

CUSINS. I thought you were determined to turn your back on the wicked side of life.

BARBARA. There is no wicked side: life is all one. And I never wanted to shirk my share in whatever evil must be endured, whether it be sin or suffering. I wish I could cure you of middle-class ideas, Dolly.

CUSINS [*gasping*] Middle cl—! A snub! A social snub to me! from the daughter of a foundling!

BARBARA. That is why I have no class, Dolly: I come straight out of the heart of the whole people. If I were middle-class I should turn my back on my father's business; and we should both live in an artistic drawing room, with you reading the reviews in one corner, and I in the other at the piano, playing Schumann: both very superior persons, and neither of us a bit of use. Sooner than that, I would sweep out these sheds, or be one of Bodger's barmaids. Do you know what would have happened if you had refused papa's offer?

CUSINS. I wonder!

BARBARA. I should have given you up and married the man who accepted it. After all, my dear old mother has more sense than any of you. I felt like her when I saw this place—felt that I must have it—that never,

never, never could I let it go ; only she thought it was the houses and the kitchen ranges and the linen and china, when it was really all the human souls to be saved : not weak souls in starved bodies, sobbing with gratitude for a scrap of bread and treacle, but fullfed, quarrelsome, snobbish, uppish creatures, all standing on their little rights and dignities, and thinking that my father ought to be greatly obliged to them for making so much money for him—and so he ought. That is where salvation is really wanted. My father shall never throw it in my teeth again that my converts were bribed with bread. [*She is transfigured*]. I have got rid of the bribe of bread. I have got rid of the bribe of heaven. Let God's work be done for its own sake : the work he had to create us to do because it cannot be done except by living men and women. When I die, let him be in my debt, not I in his ; and let me forgive him as becomes a woman of my rank.

CUSINS. Then the way of life lies through the factory of death ?

BARBARA. Yes, through the raising of hell to heaven and of man to God, through the unveiling of an eternal light in the Valley of The Shadow. [*Seizing him with both hands*] Oh, did you think my courage would never come back ? did you believe that I was a deserter ? that I, who have stood in the streets, and taken my people to my heart, and talked of the holiest and greatest things with them, could ever turn back and chatter foolishly to fashionable people about nothing in a drawing room ? Never, never, never, never : Major Barbara will die with the colors. Oh ! and I have my dear little Dolly boy still ; and he has found me my place and my work. Glory Hallelujah ! [*She kisses him*].

CUSINS. My dearest : consider my delicate health. I cannot stand as much happiness as you can.

BARBARA. Yes : it is not easy work being in love with me, is it ? But it's good for you. [*She runs to the shed, and calls, childlike*] Mamma ! Mamma ! [*Bilton comes out of the shed, followed by Undershaft*]. I want Mamma.

UNDERSHAFT. She is taking off her list slippers, dear. [*He passes on to Cusins*] Well? What does she say?

CUSINS. She has gone right up into the skies.

LADY BRITOMART [*coming from the shed and stopping on the steps, obstructing Sarah, who follows with Lomax. Barbara clutches like a baby at her mother's skirt*] Barbara: when will you learn to be independent and to act and think for yourself? I know as well as possible what that cry of " Mamma, Mamma," means. Always running to me!

SARAH [*touching Lady Britomart's ribs with her finger tips and imitating a bicycle horn*] Pip! pip!

LADY BRITOMART [*highly indignant*] How dare you say pip pip to me, Sarah? You are both very naughty children. What do you want, Barbara?

BARBARA. I want a house in the village to live in with Dolly. [*Dragging at the skirt*] Come and tell me which one to take.

UNDERSHAFT [*to Cusins*] Six o'clock tomorrow morning, Euripides.

THE END

PRINCIPAL WORKS OF BERNARD SHAW

An Unsocial Socialist, 1884
Cashel Byron's Profession, 1885–6
The Irrational Knot, 1885–7
Love Among the Artists, 1887–8
Fabian Essays in Socialism (edited), 1889
The Quintessence of Ibsenism, 1891
Widowers' Houses, 1893
The Perfect Wagnerite, 1898
Plays Pleasant and Unpleasant, 1898
The Man of Destiny, 1898
Fabianism and the Empire, 1900
Three Plays for Puritans, 1901
The Admirable Bashville, 1901
Man and Superman, 1903
Is Free Trade alive or dead?, 1906
How he Lied to her Husband, 1907
John Bull's Other Island, 1907
Major Barbara, 1907
The Sanity of Art, 1908
The Doctor's Dilemma, 1911
Getting Married, 1911
The Shewing-Up of Blanco Posnet, 1911
Commonsense about the War, 1914
Misalliance, 1914
The Dark Lady of the Sonnets, 1914
Fanny's First Play, 1914
Androcles and the Lion, Overruled, and Pygmalion, 1916
Preface to the W.E.A. Education Year Book, 1918
Great Catherine, 1919
Heartbreak House, 1919
Back to Methuselah, 1921
Saint Joan, 1924
Translations and Tomfooleries, 1926
The Intelligent Woman's Guide to Socialism, 1928
Immaturity, 1930
The Apple Cart, 1930
Doctors' Delusion, Crude Criminology, Sham Education, 1931
The Adventures of the Black Girl in her Search for God, 1932
Short Stories, Scraps, and Shavings, 1932
Too True to be Good, 1934
Village Wooing and On the Rocks, 1934
The Simpleton of the Unexpected Isles, 1936
The Six of Calais, 1936
The Millionairess, 1936
Geneva, 1939
In Good King Charles's Golden Days, 1939
Everybody's Political What's What?, 1944

THE PENGUIN SHAKESPEARE

EDITED BY G. B. HARRISON

—

Titles now available:

Hamlet – The Tempest – Twelfth Night –

The Second Part of Henry the Fourth – As You Like It –

Troylus and Cressida

Ready shortly:

Macbeth – King Lear – The Sonnets

—

The text of the Penguin Shakespeare is not a reprint of existing texts, but a new text specially prepared for this edition from the original folios and quartos. Each volume contains the following introductory matter:

1. A chronological list of Shakespeare's works;
2. A short life of Shakespeare;
3. A note on the Elizabethan theatre, with a drawing;
4. A brief introduction to the play.

There are also notes and a glossary at the end of each volume, but the distraction of notes and references in the text itself has been avoided. The notes have been considerably expanded in the course of subsequent reprints.

'... This is Shakespeare well edited and well produced; books as bright as new pins, planned with care – explanatory notes are sound and often refreshingly forthright; with the general reader in mind, the editor rightly refrains from considering too curiously. Altogether an admirable enterprise.' – *Sunday Times*.

Further plays are in preparation, and the volumes already published will be reprinted as opportunity permits.

—

THE PENGUIN CLASSICS

A LIBRARY OF NEW TRANSLATIONS

EDITED BY E.V. RIEU

HOMER: THE ODYSSEY – *Translated by E. V. Rieu*

'He catches the directness and simplicity and poise of the original better than any previous translator.' – *The Listener*

DE MAUPASSANT: BOULE DE SUIF AND OTHER STORIES
Translated by H. N. P. Sloman

'The translation has been admirably done.' – *The Scotsman*

SOPHOCLES: THE THEBAN PLAYS
Translated by E. F. Watling

'Mr Watling is to be congratulated on his success in enabling the reader to grasp the character of these great dramas.'
– *Free Verse*

VOLTAIRE: CANDIDE – *Translated by John Butt*

'Mr Butt has given a pleasing modern English translation, and an informative introduction on Voltaire's work.'
– *British Book News*

TACITUS: ON BRITAIN AND GERMANY
Translated by H. Mattingly

'Should meet with a wide public. It is exciting to think of the pleasure the Agricola and Germania can give to new readers.' – *Fortnightly Review*

IN PREPARATION

XENOPHON: THE PERSIAN EXPEDITION
Translated by Rex Warner

DANTE: THE INFERNO – *Translated by Dorothy L. Sayers*

APULEIUS: THE GOLDEN ASS – *Translated by Robert Graves*

GOETHE: FAUST – *Translated by Philip Wayne*

TURGENEV: ON THE EVE – *Translated by Gilbert Gardiner*

VIRGIL: THE PASTORAL POEMS – *Translated by E. V. Rieu*

PREVOST: MANON LESCAUT – *Translated by L. W. Tancock*

PELICAN BOOKS

A SELECTION OF RECENT ADDITIONS AND REPRINTS

*The Archaeology of Palestine – *W. Albright*	A196
Africa Emergent – *W. M. Macmillan*	A191
*The Physical Basis of Personality – *V. H. Mottram*	A139
*Mathematician's Delight – *W. W. Sawyer*	A121
*Metals in the Service of Man – *A. Street and W. Alexander*	A125
*Geology in the Service of Man – *W. G. Fearnsides and O. M. B. Bulman*	A128
Plato and His Dialogues – *G. Lowes Dickinson*	A155
*Climbing in Britain – *J. E. Q. Barford*	A160
*Fish Lore – *A. F. Magri MacMahon*	A161
*English Letters of the 18th Century – Edited by James Aitken	A163
*English Letters of the 19th Century – Edited by James Aitken	A164
The Bleak Age – *J. L. and Barbara Hammond*	A171
*A Short History of English Drama – *B. Ifor Evans*	A172
*The World's Wealth – W. G. Moore	A173
*The Irish – *Sean O'Faolain*	A184
*The Life of Jesus – *C. J. Cadoux*	A189
*An Outline of European Architecture – *N. Pevsner* [2]	A109
*Film – *R. Manvell* [2]	A126
*John Citizen and the Law – *Ronald Rubinstein*	A169
*The Population of Britain – *Eva M. Hubback*	A174
Religion and the Rise of Capitalism – *R. H. Tawney*	A23
*Ballet – *Arnold Haskell*	A122
Civilisation – *Clive Bell*	A28
*Introducing Shakespeare – *G. B. Harrison*	A43

PELICAN BOOKS – *continued*

SELECTED POEMS

T. S. Eliot

D4

Readers who are familiar only with the 'traditional' poets must revise their attitude to poetry if they are to get on terms with T. S. Eliot, the major poet of this modern age. The main poem in this collection is 'The Waste Land' (1922) to which Mr Eliot has himself supplied some revealing footnotes which help the reader to cope with the associations and allusions in which the poem is so rich. Mr Eliot himself has said 'Genuine poetry can communicate before it is understood', and in the rhythms, images and epithets of these poems there is an unmistakable and incandescent power of communication.

HASSAN

James Elroy Flecker

675

This play is based upon some old Turkish tales which James Elroy Flecker dramatised when he was working in the Middle East in 1911. It has proved one of the most spectacular plays to be seen on the modern English stage, and has been broadcast with equal success. Those who now read it for the first time in this Penguin edition will discover that, on the printed page as well, *Hassan* is a vivid evocation of the traditional splendours and enormities of ancient Bagdad.

SEVEN FAMOUS ONE ACT PLAYS

edited by J. A. Ferguson

117

This collection is eminently suitable for productions of amateur dramatic societies. It comprises comedy, tragedy, 'costume', fantasy, and character pieces, including W. W. Jacobs' famous thriller *The Monkey's Paw*, Sir Alan Herbert's lively satire *Two Gentlemen of Soho*, Alfred Sutro's *A Marriage Has Been Arranged*, *The Maker of Dreams* by Oliphant Down, *The Cloak* by Clifford Bax, Stanley Houghton's *The Dear Departed* and the Editor's own play *Campbell of Kilmohr*.